SPIKE

by Ian F   Newman

Copyright © 2022 by Ian Hislop & Nick Newman
The Goons extracts were used with the kind permission of
Spike Milligan Productions
The cover illustrations were used with the kind permission of
Spike Milligan Productions
All Rights Reserved

SPIKE is fully protected under the copyright laws of the British Commonwealth, including Canada, the United States of America, and all other countries of the Copyright Union. All rights, including professional and amateur stage productions, recitation, lecturing, public reading, motion picture, radio broadcasting, television, online/digital production, and the rights of translation into foreign languages are strictly reserved.

ISBN 978-0-573-13369-5

concordtheatricals.co.uk
concordtheatricals.com

FOR AMATEUR PRODUCTION ENQUIRIES

UNITED KINGDOM AND WORLD
EXCLUDING NORTH AMERICA
licensing@concordtheatricals.co.uk
020-7054-7298

Each title is subject to availability from Concord Theatricals, depending upon country of performance.

CAUTION: Professional and amateur producers are hereby warned that *SPIKE* is subject to a licensing fee. The purchase, renting, lending or use of this book does not constitute a licence to perform this title(s), which licence must be obtained from the appropriate agent prior to any performance. Performance of this title(s) without a licence is a violation of copyright law and may subject the producer and/or presenter of such performances to penalties. Both amateurs and professionals considering a production are strongly advised to apply to the appropriate agent before starting rehearsals, advertising, or booking a theatre. A licensing fee must be paid whether the title is presented for charity or gain and whether or not admission is charged.

This work is published by Samuel French, an imprint of Concord Theatricals Ltd.

Professional Performing Rights: applications for performance by professionals in any medium and in any language throughout the world should be addressed to Casarotto Ramsay & Associates Ltd website: www.casarotto.co.uk tel: +44 (0) 207 287 4450 email: rights@casarotto.co.uk.

No one shall make any changes in this title for the purpose of production. No part of this book may be reproduced, stored in a retrieval system, scanned, uploaded, or transmitted in any form, by any means, now known or yet to be invented, including mechanical, electronic, digital, photocopying, recording, videotaping, or otherwise, without the prior written permission of the publisher. No one shall share this title, or part of this title, to any social media or file hosting websites.

The moral right of Ian Hislop & Nick Newman to be identified as author of this work has been asserted in accordance with Section 77 of the Copyright, Designs and Patents Act 1988.

USE OF COPYRIGHTED MUSIC

A licence issued by Concord Theatricals to perform this play does not include permission to use the incidental music specified in this publication. In the United Kingdom: Where the place of performance is already licensed by the PERFORMING RIGHT SOCIETY (PRS) a return of the music used must be made to them. If the place of performance is not so licensed then application should be made to PRS for Music (www.prsformusic.com). A separate and additional licence from PHONOGRAPHIC PERFORMANCE LTD (www.ppluk.com) may be needed whenever commercial recordings are used. Outside the United Kingdom: Please contact the appropriate music licensing authority in your territory for the rights to any incidental music.

USE OF COPYRIGHTED THIRD-PARTY MATERIALS

Licensees are solely responsible for obtaining formal written permission from copyright owners to use copyrighted third-party materials (e.g., artworks, logos) in the performance of this play and are strongly cautioned to do so. If no such permission is obtained by the licensee, then the licensee must use only original materials that the licensee owns and controls. Licensees are solely responsible and liable for clearances of all third-party copyrighted materials, and shall indemnify the copyright owners of the play(s) and their licensing agent, Concord Theatricals Ltd., against any costs, expenses, losses and liabilities arising from the use of such copyrighted third-party materials by licensees.

IMPORTANT BILLING AND CREDIT REQUIREMENTS

If you have obtained performance rights to this title, please refer to your licensing agreement for important billing and credit requirements.

All performing licences have an obligation on the part of the licensee to display the following credit in all programmes for the licensee's production of the Play: "The Goons extracts were used with the kind permission of Spike Milligan Productions".

SPIKE was first presented at the Watermill Theatre, Newbury, on 27 January 2022, with the following cast:

SPIKE MILLIGAN	John Dagleish
JANET	Margaret Cabourn-Smith
PETER SELLERS	George Kemp
HARRY SECOMBE	Jeremy Lloyd
DENIS MAIN-WILSON/PETER ETON	James Mack
ELLIE MORRIS	Ellie Morris
BBC EXECUTIVE	Robert Mountford
ANNOUNCER	Stephen Fry

The touring production included

SPIKE MILLIGAN	Robert Wilfort
PETER SELLERS	Patrick Warner
MYRA	Tesni Kujore
BBC ANNOUNCER	Peter Dukes
DOCTOR	Sam Ducane

Other parts were played by members of the company.

Director	Paul Hart
Designer	Katie Lias
Composer	Tayo Akinbode
Lighting designer	Rory Beaton
Sound Designer	Tom Marshall
Associate Director	Robert Kirby
Movement Director	Anjali Mehra
Foley Sound Consultant	Ruth Sullivan
Produced by	Karl Sydow and David Parfitt

A Karl Sydow, Trademark Films, PW Productions and Watermill Theatre Production

CHARACTERS

SPIKE MILLIGAN – 35. Manic, anarchic, rebellious, troubled and troublesome comic genius who is scarred by WW2 and on the brink of changing comedy forever. With his landmark radio comedy *The Goon Show*, he is now fighting a new war with the BBC.

PETER SELLERS – 32. The man of many voices – but rarely his own. A suave, seductive film-star in the making, he is possibly as crazy as Spike.

HARRY SECOMBE – 32. A jovial extrovert and multi-talented performer – and the voice of reason in the Goons. A natural peacemaker and the rock all can turn to.

JANET – 30s. A Foley Artist producing live sound effects and general production assistant. Undervalued, underpaid and the lifeblood of the BBC – who ensures programmes are completed on time

DENIS MAIN-WILSON – 29. Exasperated but brilliant producer of the early Goon Shows, who is constantly having to defend Spike against BBC management.

JUNE – 30. Spike's half-Italian, long-suffering wife, therapist and nursemaid, who has to deal with his tantrums and depression.

PETER ETON – 34. Genial, avuncular, no-nonsense ex-drama BBC producer who supports Spike whilst standing up to him. Eton instils vital discipline in the anarchic *The Goon Show*.

BBC EXECUTIVE – 30s. Spike's BBC nemesis He is officer class and embodies all the worst traits of 1950s management including pomposity, sexism and callousness.

MAJOR JENKINS – 30s. Spike's military nemesis – embodying all the worst traits of 1940s army officers including pomposity, officiousness and callousness.

MYRA – 30s. Harry Secombe's loving and loyal wife who keeps him grounded at all times.

THE CRITICS – archetypal media pundits who earnestly compete to say more ludicrous things about *The Goon Show*. Prone to hyperbole (though the quotes featured are real).

MILDRED – 30s. The BBC Executive's repressed, more open-minded and intelligent wife.

PETER BROUGH – star radio ventriloquist with his puppet Archie.

BBC ANNOUNCER – classic plummy-voiced BBC announcer of the kind you don't hear any more.

FEMALE REPORTER – well-spoken thrusting *Radio Time*s hackette.

DOCTOR – sympathetic foil to hard-nosed Major Jenkins.

AUTHOR'S NOTES

SPIKE IN THE EYE

Spike Milligan enjoyed a long association with the magazine that gave Ian Hislop and myself our break in comedy writing.

As a cartoonist and writer for *Private Eye* for over 40 years, I've been acutely aware of Spike Milligan's presence in the magazine. Spike first appeared in *Private Eye* issue number 10, in 1962 – bewailing his statelessness in a letter trailed on the cover as 'The poet Milligan speaks.' The framed letter still hangs in the *Private Eye* offices. In his tome *Private Eye – the First 50 Years*, *Private Eye*'s historian Adam MacQueen records that Issue 11 brought better news: "I have been granted Welsh citizenship, provided I stay on a mountainside and only say 'Baa'."

Former *Private Eye* Editor Richard Ingrams recalls that "Spike was always a terrific fan of *Private Eye*. He would constantly send things in. I'd always put them in." Over the years, Spike contributed many letters and jokes to the magazine. In 1964 he wrote an entire page about the new pirate radio station Radio Caroline, entitled 'Spike Milligan Shouts Ahoy There'. He also drew cartoons. These were immensely encouraging to me as an aspiring cartoonist. The drawings were naïve at best – and showed that you didn't have to be an expert draughtsperson to be a funny cartoonist.

In 1966, when the magazine ran into financial trouble – facing enormous costs for lost libel cases – Spike helped the Eye out by performing in a benefit concert entitled 'The Rustle of Spring'. This followed a libel action by Lord Russell of Liverpool, who sued the magazine for suggesting that a book he had written about Nazi war crimes was actually pandering to salacious and sadistic tastes. It cost the magazine £5,000 damages and £3,000 costs – the equivalent of £1340,000 today. Spike performed alongside a host of names from the satire boom, including Peter Cook, Dudley Moore, John Bird, David Frost and Willie Rushton – as well as top comedians such as Peter Sellers and Bob Monkhouse.

Later, the Eye would produce Spike Milligan merchandise – such as 'Milligan's Mug' – a mug bearing four images of Spike with the caption 'The Face that launched a thousand ships.' The caption was intended to read 'The face that launched a thousand quips', but the then Art Director and designer Tony Rushton misheard Milligan down the telephone. Spike was surprisingly good-humoured about the error. Milligan also contributed to a fund-raising floppy disc 'The Sound of Talbot' in 1980 – a joke about Sir James Goldsmith's recently launched and ultimately failing *Now* magazine.

Richard Ingrams had connections with Spike which predated the Eye's launch. In 1961 he directed a production of Milligan's post-apocalyptic satire *The Bedsitting Room*, starring Willie Rushton. Says Ingrams, "Before *Private Eye* I was running a theatre company. We went to Spike and asked him to write a play. He fished out this one he'd already written, with John Antrobus. Spike didn't think it was very good." Audiences disagreed – it opened in Canterbury and transferred to the West End. Ingrams would later feature as an announcer alongside Eye contributor John Wells in Spike's 'Q' TV series – and although he wasn't a fan of the *Goon Show*, Ingrams saw Spike as a genius. Ingrams wrote in the Guardian, "Like many men of genius Spike went through life nourishing a resentment that his talents were not sufficiently appreciated. In Spike's case, the special focus of his hostility was the BBC." *Private Eye* staff were familiar with Spike ringing up out of the blue and cursing down the line about his treatment by the Corporation.

Spike's interest in the magazine also reflected his respect for the Eye's proprietor Peter Cook, who bought the magazine in 1962 after starring in the hit satirical revue Beyond the Fringe. The admiration was mutual. When at school at Radley, Cook would feign illness to gain access to the school sanatorium on a Friday night, in order to listen to the *Goon Show* on the wireless. In 1955, aged 17, Cook wrote a radio script which was rejected by the BBC because it was too similar to *The Goons*. So similar was it that the BBC's Peter Titherdge pointed out that it was actually a very good Goon script – and it eventually landed on Spike's desk. Milligan was so impressed that he invited Cook up to lunch in London. Quite what Spike made of the schoolboy when he arrived is unknown – and sadly neither Cook nor Milligan could subsequently remember what was discussed, according to Cook's biographer Harry Thompson. When at Cambridge, Cook wrote sketches for Footlights student revues that were infused with Milligan influences. Characters such as F.Nidgcombe, Arthur Frad and Larry Splutt bear all the hallmarks of the Goons.

Over the next 40 years Cook and Milligan would work together sporadically – appearing on each other's TV shows and in films together. They even collaborated on a 'Beyond the Fringe meets The Goons' project – a parody of 'Bridge Over the River Kwai' entitled *Bridge Over the River Wye* – in which Cook and Jonathan Miller performed alongside Milligan and Peter Sellers. While Cook was celebrated as a savage satirist, his contributions to the Eye were often Milliganesque nonsense pieces involving large killer bees.

So Spike's spirit loomed large over *Private Eye*. Ingrams's successor as *Private Eye* Editor – my colleague Ian Hislop – had his own encounter with Spike in the mid 1980s when he interviewed Spike for Radio 4's 'Midweek' radio show. "Spike was the birthday guest, and in those days they were presented with a bottle of champagne." Says Ian. "It was live and on air, and I opened the bottle only for it to explode all over my notes written in green ink, which left me with an unreadable sea of green. Spike thought it hilarious, and he helped me out by interviewing himself, asking himself questions. He loved things going wrong. He loved the anarchy."

Spike's most celebrated association with the Eye was when he placed a lonely hearts advertisement in the small ads at the back of the magazine. It read 'Spike Milligan seeks rich, well-insured widow. Intention: murder.' He received 48 replies.

Nick Newman

ACT ONE

Scene One

(A 1950s BBC radio studio. We see an empty stage apart from a desk full of interesting and strange objects. There are a pair of shoes, a miniature door frame, an umbrella, a pile of audio tape, a biscuit tin, a swanee whistle, a ruler, a hot water bottle, a series of buzzers and bells on a board, and a pair of coconut shells. There is a also a tray full of gravel and a record player for playing 78 rpm discs. **JANET** *the foley artist and sound effects wizard enters to address the audience.)*

JANET. The BBC Sound Effects Department is the finest in the world. Its job is to produce convincing representations of a wide range of audio experiences for both radio drama and comedy on the Home Service and Light programme. We often perform live during recordings and it is the job of the spot effects operator to illustrate the narrative with suitable noises. So when Special Agent Dick Barton makes a routine call to a suspicious house we hear his footsteps up the drive way...

(She puts the shoes on her hands and crunches them on the gravel tray...)

...then he rings the doorbell...

(She rings a bell on the tray...)

Only to find that when the door opens...

> *(She makes the sound of door opening dragging a ruler across a ridged hot water bottle.)*

It's the lair of the heavily armed master criminal who shoots at him...

> *(She makes a twanging sound with a ruler.)*

...with his bow and arrow. So Dick has to make a run for it...

> *(She puts the shoes on her hands again and rapidly recreates a running sound...)*

...through the bushes...

> *(She rustles the audio tape.)*

... Startling some birds who fly away...

> *(She opens and closes the umbrella.)*

...then crashing into some dustbins...

> *(She shakes the biscuit tin full of broken glass and coins.)*

Before finally making his escape... on a horse...

> *(She picks up the coconuts and makes a galloping noise, fading into the distance.)*

So all totally convincing... but sometimes we need something more sophisticated to transport the listener out of their cosy living room into another world. The BBC is of course at the forefront of technological advances.

> *(She unveils a very elderly looking gramophone player.)*

...and has the largest sound effects library in the world, with thousands of different noise-scapes all stored on the latest 78 rpm acetate discs.

(She gets out a few discs...)

We have everything from a cistercian monastery...

(We hear echoey chanting...)

To an Ethiopian village market...

(We hear chickens, goats and cries of villagers.)

To complete silence...

(We hear nothing at all.)

And that is just one of the eleven types of silence we have – office silence, desert silence, silence in a theatre...

(She plays the 'silence' which is interrupted by a cough.)

...typical! And at the other end of the audiological spectrum we have explosions. From small to large, from civilian to military, from a domestic boiler to an Atom bomb. They are all here neatly catalogued and filed. We've provided the effects for thousands and of radio shows broadcasting across the world, and we have had very very few complaints.

*(Enter **SPIKE** with an acetate record.)*

SPIKE. I would like to complain.

JANET. Not again Mr. Milligan. What is it this time?

SPIKE. This explosion – it's not loud enough...

JANET. It is **pretty** loud Mr Milligan.

SPIKE. No, no – it's got to be much **much** louder – this sounds like a bloody raspberry!

JANET. It's Disc 17, Side A track 8 – Explosions, heavy, mortar.

> (**JANET** *shows him the LP record from which the sound effect is taken. A* **BBC EXECUTIVE** *appears.*)

BBC EXECUTIVE. What appears to be the problem?

JANET. Mr Milligan is unhappy with the sound of the bomb going off.

BBC EXECUTIVE. Well let's hear it.

> (*She plays the record with the bomb effect. It is quite loud. They both jump.* **SPIKE** *remains unmoved.*)

SPIKE. Whoever thinks that sounds like a mortar must be deaf.

JANET. Possibly from listening to it.

SPIKE. I am telling you that is not a mortar bomb. I **do** know what I'm talking about!

Scene Two

(The lights suddenly change and we hear a soundscape of gunfire. The **BBC EXECUTIVE** *puts on an army cap to become* **MAJOR JENKINS** *and* **SPIKE** *puts on a tin helmet to become his former self. We are suddenly back in Italy in 1944.)*

MAJOR JENKINS. Bombardier Milligan – make yourself useful.

SPIKE. Sir!

MAJOR JENKINS. We need to get fresh batteries and a twenty two radio set up to the observation post.

SPIKE. Where exactly sir?

MAJOR JENKINS. OP 1 is straight up there beyond the burnt out Sherman tank.

(He points up the hill.)

SPIKE. Right away Sir. Is it always this quiet?

MAJOR JENKINS. Welcome to Monte Cassino.

SPIKE. You're welcome to it too.

MAJOR JENKINS. Put a sock in it Milligan and get on with it.

SPIKE. *(To* **SOLDIERS.***)* Ballard, Birch, you're coming with me.

*(***TWO SOLDIERS** *in tin hats appear.)*

BALLARD. Why?

SPIKE. You just volunteered.

BIRCH. Where are we going?

*(***SPIKE** *consults map.)*

SPIKE. Apparently World War Two is that way

> (**SPIKE** *points up the hill.*)

We will go up the stone-lined gully.

When it ends we start climbing the hill – you can see it's all terraced for olive trees. And if they start mortaring don't get stuck in the bloody gully or you'll get yourself killed... which is against regulations.

> (**BALLARD** *and* **BIRCH** *smile.* **SPIKE** *and the two soldiers start inching up the hillside. We hear a small mortar. Then more shells exploding.*)

BALLARD. They've seen us!

SPIKE. And I don't think they like us.

> (*Another explosion.*)

BIRCH. We're sitting ducks.

SPIKE. I hope we're insured.

> (*Another mortar explodes much closer to them.*)

Get down!

> (*They lie flat on the ground.* **SPIKE** *fumbles for a woodbine.*)

I'm dying...

BIRCH. What?

SPIKE. ...for a fag!

> (*Suddenly there is a whizz and an enormous bang right on top of them. Blackout.*)

Scene Three

(A **BBC ANNOUNCER** *appears behind a large microphone, wearing a black tie and dinner jacket.)*

ANNOUNCER. This is the BBC, but that's not my fault.

You're listening to the steam driven, technicolour *Goon Show*!

(We hear Goon show theme and three performers take the stage.)

Mr Harry Secombe! Comic and tenor, but a fiver will do.

*(***SECOMBE** *is rotund, and sports a small bow tie. He comes on stage with a leek, as if it were a cigar and blows a raspberry.)*

Mr Peter Sellers, the man of many voices.

(Bespectacled **SELLERS** *comes on stage. We hear a sound effect of a huge crowd going wild and then cut off suddenly.)*

And least but not last, Mr Spike Milligan!

(Sound effect of a drum roll. **SPIKE** *walks on backwards, facing the wrong way and bows to the back of the stage. Then turns round.)*

And this week's episode is entitled... 'We don't appear to have a title Denis'.

SECOMBE. Good title!

(Enter **PRODUCER, DENIS MAIN-WILSON.***)*

MAIN-WILSON. Is it too much to ask for a title?

SPIKE. You've got a title. Producer. Isn't that good enough?

SELLERS. How about Esteemed Producer?

MAIN-WILSON. A steamed up producer might be more accurate.

SPIKE. *(Smiles and puts on a silly voice.)* I write the jokes Denis.

MAIN-WILSON. Really? That's very reassuring. Then perhaps you could get on and finish the script? By this evening would be good. Because that's when the recording is.

SPIKE. Don't worry Denis, it's all up here!

(Points to his head.)

MAIN-WILSON. It would be quite nice if it were down here.

(Points to script.)

SPIKE. I've had an idea...

MAIN-WILSON. Good.

SPIKE. Let's go to the pub!

Scene Four

*(We are in Grafton's Pub. **SPIKE**, **SECOMBE** and **SELLERS** are having a noisy drinking/ideas session. The atmosphere is chaotic but convivial – the banter is vaguely logical and competitive. Old friends relaxed in each other's company, trying voices, characters. A lot of smoking.)*

SELLERS. *(To **SECOMBE**.)* Your round Mr. Seagoon.

SECOMBE. How dare you. I am not round. I am just well-built. I have a fuller figure.

SPIKE. It's fuller batter pudding.

*(**SELLERS** wears a flash suit and adopts a posh voice.)*

SELLERS. I would buy a drink but I don't appear to have any money I'm frightfully sorry.

SECOMBE. You're not sorry.

SELLERS. You're right. I'm not sorry at all, I'm glad do you hear me? I'm Glad!

SPIKE. You're not Glad. She works in Lyons Corner House – you're an impostor. Police! Arrest this man!

SELLERS. You'll never take me alive.

(He mimes putting a gun to his head.)

SPIKE. Don't do it!

SELLERS. All right I won't. Largely because my fingers aren't loaded.

SPIKE. If you're trying to make fools of the police you're too late! They were fools long before you got here. Hang on while I write that down...

*(He scribbles a joke down on the back of a beer mat. **BARMAID** interrupts.)*

BARMAID. Is anyone actually going to buy a drink?

SECOMBE. Well if you insist, sir, I'll have a pint of your finest brandy...

*(Enter **MAIN-WILSON** looking distraught.)*

MAIN-WILSON. Look is there **any** sign of a finished script?

SPIKE. It's the man from the BBC! You're just in time!

MAIN-WILSON. For what?

SPIKE. For your arrival.

MAIN-WILSON. Do you know what the time is?

SPIKE. Yes, I've got it written on this piece of paper.

MAIN-WILSON. What?

SPIKE. If anybody asks me the time, I can show it to them.

*(**SPIKE** takes a piece of paper out of his pocket and shows it to **MAIN-WILSON**.)*

MAIN-WILSON. But it says here that it's eight o'clock.

SPIKE. That's right when I wrote it down, it was eight o'clock.

MAIN-WILSON. Hang on. Supposing when somebody asks you the time, it isn't eight o'clock?

SPIKE. Then I don't show it to them.

MAIN-WILSON. Well how do you know when it's eight o'clock?

SPIKE. I've got it written down on a piece of paper!

MAIN-WILSON. Very funny Spike. But in actual fact it's half past five and the show starts at seven.

(**SELLERS** *picks up the piece of paper.*)

SELLERS. *(Cockney geezer voice.)* You've been ripped off guv! This piece of paper isn't working.

(**SPIKE** *holds it to his ear and listens to it.*)

SPIKE. You're right! It's stopped! At precisely eight o'clock!

(**MAIN-WILSON** *is amused, but exasperated.*)

MAIN-WILSON. Spike, you have GOT to be more punctual!

SPIKE. Don't worry. I'm getting one of those new things that my Grandad has. It wakes you up at eight o'clock, boils the kettle, and pours a cup of tea.

MAIN-WILSON. You mean a teasmaid?

SPIKE. No, my Grandma.

(*All cheer.* **MAIN-WILSON** *tries to maintain control.* **SPIKE** *is scribbling the jokes down on a scrap of paper.*)

MAIN-WILSON. Come on boys, we can't afford to upset the BBC.

SELLERS. You would say that – you're wearing a BBC suit.

SECOMBE. How can you tell?

SELLERS. Small checks.

MAIN-WILSON. *(Wearily.)* All right, I'll get the drinks.

(**SECOMBE** *blows a raspberry.*)

Scene Five

*(A **BBC** office. We see a **BBC EXECUTIVE** with a moustache, pipe and blazer sitting behind a desk. He is fiddling with a phone system he cannot work.)*

BBC EXECUTIVE. Sorry I lost you – is that the switchboard? No? Who am I talking to? The shipping forecast... how did that happen?

*(He notices **MAIN-WILSON**.)*

Sorry Denis. Trying to get us a cup of tea. Having a problem getting to grips with this new-fangled gizmo...

*(**BBC EXECUTIVE** gives up with the telephone and goes to the door and shouts.)*

Three teas please Miss er...

*(**MAIN-WILSON** has clearly been hauled up in front of the **BBC EXECUTIVE** and the tone is headmasterly.)*

MAIN-WILSON. Two actually. Spike says he's going to be a bit late

BBC EXECUTIVE. Well what a surprise. Now look here Denis. I've had a series of complaints from the Sound Effects wallahs about your man Milligan. Not to put too fine a point on it, he is becoming a pain in the proverbial.

MAIN-WILSON. Spike is a perfectionist. He's trying to do something new in comedy.

BBC EXECUTIVE. Oh dear. I hope you are doing your best to discourage him. What the listeners want to hear is something familiar. Like Educating Archie?

MAIN-WILSON. The ventriloquist act?

BBC EXECUTIVE. That's the chap. Ventriloquism on radio. First rate. You can't see the lips move.

*(Enter **JANET** the production assistant with tea on a tray.)*

Thank you... er... Sandra?

JANET. Janet... and if you need me again its extension forty five, then press 'call'.

(She shows him the buttons to press.)

BBC EXECUTIVE. *(Laughing off his inadequacy.)* You girls will be running everything soon...

*(**JANET** looks unconvinced.)*

JANET. Really?

MAIN-WILSON. Thank you Janet.

(She exits.)

What Spike wants to do, and the boys are all with him, is a show that is a bit less traditional and a bit more unconventional...

BBC EXECUTIVE. Well that's no excuse for being confused and loud and having no decent curtain lines to end the sketches. It's all too... crazy.

MAIN-WILSON. Originally you insisted on calling the show Crazy People.

BBC EXECUTIVE. I didn't mean literally... we did want to call it Crazy People but then we found out there already was a show at the Palladium called Crazy People so management had a long think and we came up with the rather brilliant alternative of... Young Crazy People.

MAIN-WILSON. Didn't really catch on did it?

BBC EXECUTIVE. I still think it was a better title than *The Goon Show*. Which doesn't mean anything. The

Deputy Head of Entertainment Finance thought it was pronounced "The Go On Show".

MAIN-WILSON. ...though he didn't want it to go on did he?

BBC EXECUTIVE. No, but the problem as we see it is with the balance of the team. It's quite clear who the star of the show is... Harry Secombe.

MAIN-WILSON. *(Surprised.)* Harry?

BBC EXECUTIVE. Secombe's the finished article. Solid entertainer, most amusing, thoroughly reliable – and he can sing!

MAIN-WILSON. Well, yes...

BBC EXECUTIVE. I saw him at the Windmill doing his shaving routine... very, very funny.

*(Onstage we see **SECOMBE** doing his shaving routine.)*

SECOMBE. Here's a small boy shaving for the first time...

(He begins to sing to himself in a silly voice whilst covering his face in foam with a brush and then shaving it off. Foam goes everywhere and he ends up drinking the mug of soapy water.)

(Back to the office.)

MAIN-WILSON. Harry's great, but the others are equally talented...

BBC EXECUTIVE. Yes, Sellers is awfully good. 'The Man of Many Voices' ...his impressions are first rate. On Variety Bandbox we had him doing a radio pantomime in which he did all the characters himself...

*(Onstage **SELLERS** is in the spotlight and does impressions at a rapid rate.)*

SELLERS. *(As Max Miller.)* I'm Max Miller, lady, the cheeky chappie. Now here's a funny thing, I'm so tired. You know why? I've been shoplifting – and some of those shops are really heavy.

(Audience laugh.)

Hello I'm Ted Ray. So I said to my wife "I'm going to Paris". What are you going to use for money, she said, I said "Francs", "That's no use," she said, "Frank's not going..."

(Spotlight off SELLERS. Back to the office.)

MAIN-WILSON. Peter's a very good mimic, but he is dependent on the quality of his material...

BBC EXECUTIVE. Do you know during the war Sellers used to go into the Officer's mess and passed himself off as a Major!

Even though he wasn't officer class at all, obviously...

MAIN-WILSON. We're trying to use Peter in a slightly more ambitious way, and he plays very well off Spike.

BBC EXECUTIVE. Shame you lost Michael Bentine. Very clever. Speaks several languages. Saw him doing his mad professor routine...

(He adopts a silly mid-european accent.)

Today I vill be givink my lekture in my native tongue – Slobodian... Glurnky densch shnurdling vakishnosh...

MAIN-WILSON. That's awfully good, but Bentine has gone onto other things...

BBC EXECUTIVE. Pity. I thought Bentine was the brains behind the group. Ex-RAF intelligence, you know. Plus he went to Eton.

MAIN-WILSON. And that's important is it, for performing radio comedy?

BBC EXECUTIVE. What's important, Denis, and I can't stress this enough, is that the secret of zany comedy is professionalism.

MAIN-WILSON. Professionalism?

BBC EXECUTIVE. That's the problem with your Mr Milligan. Unprofessional. Slapdash. It's like all that jazz he plays. I would say he's a better trumpeter than a comedian.

> *(Onstage* **SPIKE** *in the spotlight plays a burst of* **[WHEN THE SAINTS COME MARCHING IN]** *on the trumpet, brilliantly.)*

SPIKE. And now, for the next number – Six!

> *(Spotlight fades. Back to the office.)*

MAIN-WILSON. There's more to Spike than just a musician who can tell a few jokes. He's a one-off.

BBC EXECUTIVE. Is he? Since he's still not here I might as well tell you that of the three of them we don't really see where Milligan fits in...

MAIN-WILSON. He does write it...

BBC EXECUTIVE. Not all of it. There are other writers... you know... whatsisname and... er... the other ones...

MAIN-WILSON. You mean Jimmy Grafton, Larry Stephens, Eric Sykes...

BBC EXECUTIVE. *(Wearily and dismissively.)* Yes, writers...

MAIN-WILSON. But Spike is special – the world of the Goons is Spike's unique voice, and if...

BBC EXECUTIVE. Don't get carried away Denis. This is show business not splitting the atom. As an artiste, Milligan's just not in the same league as Secombe and Sellers. He is what you might call a 'freak' contributor.

> *(***SPIKE*** enters.)*

SPIKE. Knock knock.

BBC EXECUTIVE. Ah, Mr Milligan, at last, come in...

SPIKE. I already have.

BBC EXECUTIVE. Yes, very good. Do you know what time it is?

SPIKE. Yes. I've got it written down here on a piece of paper.

EXECUTIVE. What?

MAIN-WILSON. No Spike, now isn't the time!

SPIKE. It is according to this piece *(Of paper.)* ...

MAIN-WILSON. *(Sternly.)* Put it away Spike.

BBC EXECUTIVE. Now, Mr Milligan, enough of this foolery. I asked you here to talk about your '*Goon Show*'? What exactly **is** a 'goon'? Is it a hired thug?

SPIKE. No, it's...

BBC EXECUTIVE. Is it something to do with 'Rangoon'?

MAIN-WILSON. There's a character in the American cartoon 'Popeye' called 'Goon', but that's not important...

SPIKE. No, no – it IS important. A goon is an idiot. Someone who doesn't understand anything.

*(The **BBC EXECUTIVE** looks puzzled.)*

BBC EXECUTIVE. I'm not with you.

SPIKE. A goon is really stupid, with a hairy head, a bulbous nose and one brain cell.

MAIN-WILSON. I like the word 'Goon'. It's funny.

SPIKE. You see, Goon's a word we used in the army.

BBC EXECUTIVE. Yes, there's an awful lot about the army in the show, isn't there?

SPIKE. Is that a problem?

BBC EXECUTIVE. We feel we've had enough of the war.

SPIKE. That's what I said in 1943!

BBC EXECUTIVE. Don't start, Mr Milligan…

SPIKE. I didn't start anything! That was Hitler!

BBC EXECUTIVE. Yes, but it was all over years ago.

SPIKE. **Eight** years ago.

BBC EXECUTIVE. And you're still banging on about it.

SPIKE. There was a lot of banging as I recall.

BBC EXECUTIVE. Well there are far too many bangs in the show. I find it far too noisy.

SPIKE. Then stand further away from the wireless!

BBC EXECUTIVE. Now listen here Milligan, I'm not liking your attitude.

> *(Suddenly, the* **BBC EXECUTIVE** *becomes an* **ARMY MAJOR** *putting on an army* **OFFICER***'s cap and* **SPIKE** *is back in a surreal replay of the war.)*

BBC EXECUTIVE/MAJOR. It's all very well being bolshy, Milligan, but we won't tolerate you questioning your superiors. Nobody likes a barrack room clever-dick. And lounging around playing the trumpet and making silly jokes isn't going to win us the war.

SPIKE. Do you think a bassoon would be better? Or maybe a tuba?

BBC EXECUTIVE/MAJOR. Are you looking for seven days' detention?

SPIKE. No I'm looking for a man with a small black moustache.

BBC EXECUTIVE/MAJOR. Are you listening to a word I'm saying Milligan?

*(Suddenly we are back in the BBC office with the **BBC EXECUTIVE**, who takes off the hat.)*

BBC EXECUTIVE. Mr Milligan? Are you listening to a word I'm saying?

SPIKE. No sir!

MAIN-WILSON. He's joking of course. What Spike means is that he will very much be taking your views on board in the forthcoming programmes.

SPIKE. Is that what I mean?

MAIN-WILSON. Yes it is Spike.

Scene Six

(**MAIN-WILSON** *leads* **SPIKE** *off to the other side of the stage where he feeds in the paper and places* **SPIKE***'s reluctant hands on the typewriter keys. Slowly* **SPIKE** *starts to type to the sound of* **[FLIGHT OF THE BUMBLEBEE]**. *During this* **MAIN-WILSON** *treats him like a prize-fighting boxer.* **MAIN-WILSON** *massages his shoulders, gives him drink, mops his brow, slaps him around the face to keep him going, gives him a lighted cigarette and eventually half an orange.* **SPIKE** *carries on typing furiously, building to a crescendo when he pulls out a sheet of paper. He reads it, laughs and then screws it up and throws it into the darkness. The lights reveal a huge mountain of screwed up pieces of paper.* **SPIKE** *types again, the music repeats – and this time he is satisfied. He rips the paper out and hurries to the other side of the stage where the others are waiting for a read through.)*

Scene Seven

(BBC Theatre. The team are sitting round a table, ready for a table-read of the script. Production Assistant and Spot Effects Performer **JANET** *has a stopwatch and will be timing the read through, whilst also creating live sound effects on the sound effects table. She is trying a few out, banging, crashing and clanging.)*

SECOMBE. Still no sign of him?

SELLERS. *(Silly Clouseau-style voice.)* Ze strange case of ze disappearing Milligan. Whenever ze deadline is near... pouff...he vanishes into ze thin air...

SECOMBE. *(Trying to jolly him along.)* He's a man of mystery.

SELLERS. Yessss... ze mystery is why we put up with him!

*(**JANET**'s sound effect makes a loud clang.)*

(Normal voice.) What's that supposed to be?

JANET. Big Ben falling off Beachy Head.

SELLERS. Of course, how stupid of me.

*(**JANET** uses a balloon to make a deflating farty noise.)*

SECOMBE. And that?

JANET. The explosion of the Hindenberg. I'm working on it.

*(Enter **SPIKE**, dishevelled, to an ironic cheer.)*

MAIN-WILSON. You're late Spike.

SPIKE. I'm the late Spike Milligan.

SELLERS. Being dead would at least be a reasonable excuse.

SPIKE. Don't blame me – blame the muse.

SELLERS. What happened to her?

SPIKE. She missed her bus.

MAIN-WILSON. *(Wearily.)* Shall we give it a trundle?

> *(He hands out the scripts that **SPIKE** has produced. They all try and make sense of the extra pages that **SPIKE** has brought in.)*

SELLERS. I'm sorry Spike, I'm going to have to stop you right there.

SPIKE. What have I done now?

SELLERS. Nothing you've done. You're wearing green. I did ask that no one wears green.

SPIKE. You can't be serious!

SELLERS. My spirit guide says I can't perform with anyone wearing green. It's unlucky.

SPIKE. Your spirit guide?

SELLERS. He talks through my clairvoyant.

SPIKE. And he talks through his arse.

SECOMBE. *(Trying to smooth over the row.)* Does he work for the BBC?

MAIN-WILSON. Are you adamant about this Peter?

SELLERS. Sorry Denis, either Spike's sweater goes or I do.

> *(All look at each other uneasily, but he's deadly serious. **SPIKE** removes his green sweater.)*

SPIKE. And they say I'm nuts!

SELLERS. They said Napoleon was nuts.

*(**SECOMBE** and **SPIKE** laugh.)*

But he wasn't.

SPIKE. What?

SELLERS. I know – because I was there at Waterloo.

*(Pause as they all clock **SELLERS**' latest superstitious claim.)*

SECOMBE. Me too! Only my train was cancelled! Furtang! Furtang!

*(Once again **SECOMBE** has defused the situation.)*

Good, now that's cleared up, where are we?

JANET. We are in an army camp in deepest Bexhill.

SPIKE. That's a British army camp , not a French army camp in 1815.

*(**SELLERS** ignores the jibe.)*

MAIN-WILSON. We're on page seventeen, if anyone's interested.

(They find their places in the script.)

Peter, you're Major Bloodnock

SELLERS. *(As **BLOODNOCK**.)* You man…

*(As **SELLERS**.)*

Sorry, what's my motivation here?

MAIN-WILSON. *(Checking watch.)* Your motivation is to get through the scene as quickly as possible since due to the late arrival of the script we only have one hour until the recording. Spike, you are Bloodnock's batman.

*(They begin the sketch. **JANET** begins with steps, using the shoes on the table.)*

SELLERS. *(As **BLOODNOCK**.)* You man!

SPIKE. *(In the voice of **ECCLES**.)* Yes Major Bloodnock sir?

SELLERS. You. Take my boots off!

*(**SPIKE** makes grunting noises. **JANET** produces a squealing sound using a rubber hot water bottle.)*

SPIKE. That's one... and that's the other.

SELLERS/BLOODNOCK. Now, don't let me catch you wearing my boots again!

*(**SELLERS** and **SPIKE** corpse. **SECOMBE** laughs loudly.)*

MAIN-WILSON. Let's move onto the next scene...

SPIKE. Any notes?

MAIN-WILSON. Can you try not to look as though you're having more fun than the audience.

SELLERS. *(Laughing.)* But we can't help it. We **are**!

SECOMBE. So who am I playing now, Spike?

SPIKE. You're playing yourself. An idiot.

SECOMBE. Typecast again!

SELLERS. And me?

SPIKE. You're playing a variety of roles, all of whom happen to be idiots.

JANET. What about the women's parts?

SPIKE. We can't mention women's parts we won't get past the censor!

JANET. *(Ignoring him.)* Beryl Reid and June Whitfield are very good.

SPIKE. I think we'll do the women ourselves. It'll be funnier.

SELLERS. Agreed.

SECOMBE. Much funnier.

MAIN-WILSON. It'll certainly be cheaper.

SELLERS. I see none of my ideas seem to have made it into the script.

SPIKE. Well they might do if you bothered to write any of them down!

SELLERS. **You** write the ideas down – and then you claim that they're yours!

(There is an awkward silence.)

SECOMBE. Sound effect – Awkward Silence!

*(The other two laugh. **SECOMBE** has restored the mood again.)*

JANET. Funny lot you comedians.

SECOMBE. Let's hope so.

MAIN-WILSON. *(Increasingly exasperated.)* Back to the read through, please? Spike, you're playing Minnie Bannister? Peter, you be the policeman.

*(**JANET** opens and closes the door.)*

SELLERS/POLICEMAN. What seems to be the problem madam?

SPIKE/MIN. My husband's dead.

SELLERS/POLICEMAN. Are you sure?

*(**JANET** uses wood blocks from her tray to create a loud bang.)*

SPIKE/MIN. Yes.

SECOMBE. And the Oscar for best actor goes to Mister Harry Secombe for his non-speaking role as The Corpse! Now, time for ME, Neddie Seagoon, the hero of the hour, who arrives just in time to... hang on my script seems to be missing the final page...

SPIKE. Don't worry – it's on its way.

SELLERS. Where is it exactly?

SPIKE. It's on the same bus as the Muse

MAIN-WILSON. So long as it doesn't end with yet another huge explosion...

> *(We hear a huge explosion. Lights go out. We see the* **ANNOUNCER.***)*

ANNOUNCER. That was *The Goon Show*, a BBC recorded programme featuring Peter Sellers, Harry Secombe, and Spike Milligan with the Ray Ellington Quartet, Max Geldray and the Orchestra conducted by Wally Stott...

Scene Eight

(BBC green room. We hear audience applause off. When the lights come up we are post-show.)

*(**BBC EXECUTIVE** is there, self consciously with **MRS BBC EXECUTIVE** a woman with big glasses. They clearly didn't find the show funny. **MAIN-WILSON** arrives.)*

MAIN-WILSON. I thought that was terrific!

BBC EXECUTIVE. Really? Not too chaotic for you? Mildred and I had some difficulty following what was going on.

MILDRED. No, I just thought some of it was a bit fast.

BBC EXECUTIVE. And you didn't like those silly voices, did you?

MILDRED. Well, I ...

BBC EXECUTIVE. And as for all those vulgar raspberries...

*(Enter **SECOMBE**, blowing a raspberry.)*

SECOMBE. I thangyou!

*(Enter **SPIKE** with bottle of brandy.)*

SPIKE. *(To **BBC EXECUTIVE**.)* So what did you think?

MAIN-WILSON. They loved it!

(They look confused.)

MILDRED. I **did** like the music...

SPIKE. *(Disappointed.)* That's the only bit I didn't write...

*(She spots **SELLERS** and snubs **SPIKE**.)*

MILDRED. Oh look Maurice – there's Peter Sellers. Darling, you must introduce me... he's really becoming quite famous. I read that he's in films!

BBC EXECUTIVE. Peter, may I introduce...

SELLERS. *(Very seductively to* **MILDRED.***)* You are the most ravishing creature I've ever set eyes on. Tell me you'll steal away with me this very hour and we'll take the night train to Istanbul for a night of passion to rival anything in the Arabian Nights.

BBC EXECUTIVE. Mildred, I think it's time we left... leave these creative types to it...

(To **MAIN-WILSON.***)*

The trouble is, Denis, is that studio audiences will laugh at anything. I just don't think it's funny... or clever.

(We hear pompous classical theme music of **[THE CRITICS]**.*)*

Scene Nine

(Radio Arts Studio. Two earnest men and an earnest woman discuss the show.)

CRITIC 1 (NOEL). Welcome to the Critics, and tonight we're discussing the Home Service's popular radio entertainment, '*The Goon Show*'. Roger, are you a 'Goonie'?

CRITIC 2 (ROGER). Well, yes, Noel, I liked it very much… for me it was surrealism in sound…

CRITIC 1. Hermione?

CRITIC 3 (HERMIONE). …Yes, there are obvious influences one can detect…the whole English nonsense tradition – I can distinctly hear the voice of Edward Lear and Lewis Carroll…

CRITIC 2. …with an absurdist undertone – I'm thinking of Ionesco… Brecht… Pirandello…

CRITIC 1. Oh yes indeed… and the humour is wonderfully classless, crossing all sorts of cultural boundaries…

CRITIC 2. And the foolery… the sort of ersatz lunacy, if you will, carries a very sane message to a very mad world.

CRITIC 3. That is the whole point, is it not? *The Goon Show* is essentially shell shock on radio.

CRITIC 2. That's very good Hermione. And all those explosions, it is as if every joke ends with a literal 'boom boom'.

(All laugh in erudite chorus.)

Scene Ten

(BBC office. **SPIKE** *is yet again arguing with the management.)*

BBC EXECUTIVE. No I'm afraid I didn't hear it Spike.

Tuesday is Mildred's bridge night and I have to make myself scarce… usually go the club.

*(***JANET** *enters.)*

JANET. There's a transcript of the Critics in *The Listener*. They really do like the Goons. I thought you'd like to read it.

(Hands him a magazine. He surveys it bad temperedly for a while.)

SPIKE. Surely, now we've done enough to merit a better time slot and a repeat?

BBC EXECUTIVE. We've heard all this before Spike.

SELLERS. So it's a repeat! Success!

*(***JANET** *laughs.)*

BBC EXECUTIVE. Thank you Janice.

(He hands back the magazine. She exits.)

One shouldn't take too much notice of what the Critics say. If we did that we wouldn't have a single entertainment programme on the BBC! They didn't even like *Ray's A Laugh* with Ted Ray. I mean it had that other chap Kenneth Connor playing a character called Sidney Mincing. It was Mildred's favourite.

SPIKE. Was it really?

BBC EXECUTIVE. One thing I've learned in this business Spike is all that matters is whether THEY like it out there. The listeners. Not The Listener. *(Shouting off.)* Alice! Have we had any response to *The Goon Show*?

JANET. *(Offstage.)* Well, we have had a few letters.

BBC EXECUTIVE. A **few** letters? Oh dear.

> (**JANET** *enters with an enormous postbag which she plonks on his desk.*)

JANET. There are hundreds and hundreds of them...

SPIKE. It took me hours to write them all!

> (**JANET** *laughs.*)

BBC EXECUTIVE. Are they from children? My nephew seems to find it somewhat amusing.

JANET. No, they're from generals, charladies, bus drivers, vicars...

BBC EXECUTIVE. Oh. Really?

JANET. It's incredible. Listen to this one.

> *(She reads out.)*

"This show has influenced my husband and myself to act a little crazier when we meet our friends – and we find we enjoy life all the more!"

SPIKE. Poor friends!

BBC EXECUTIVE. But it's the listening figures that count.

JANET. The listening figures have gone up from 370,000 to 1.8 million.

BBC EXECUTIVE. It's not **all** about the figures...

JANET. Here's another one.

> *(She reads letter.)*

"The high spirits of the Goons are very infectious. Many times I chuckle into my knitting".

BBC EXECUTIVE. Says who?

JANET. That's the wife of a tax inspector.

SPIKE. I owe her. And him.

JANET. There's more...

> (**BBC EXECUTIVE** *exits in panic.*)

She continues... "The pure fantasy of this show is a perfect answer to the blues."

SPIKE. I really must listen to it. Perhaps it could help me!

Scene Eleven

(A Pub. **SECOMBE** *and* **SPIKE** *are drinking.* **BARMAID** *walks past.)*

BARMAID. I thought you lot would be on the champagne!

*(***SECOMBE** *and* **SPIKE** *raise their glasses.)*

SECOMBE. We've cracked it Spike!

SPIKE. Have we?

SECOMBE. They love us! And they love what you write! Here's to you, you mad bastard!

*(***SPIKE** *is accosted by a boring male fan.)*

FAN 1. You're those Goon chaps aren't you? Off the radio?

SPIKE. No we just sound like them.

FAN 1. You see I wasn't sure at first. But the children kept on about how amusing it was then even the wife came around, and now we just won't miss it...

SPIKE. Thank you very much.

FAN 1. And my brother-in-law who lives in Canada is an absolute addict – you might say a 'Goonatic', and his sister says that even in Australia...

SPIKE. Thank you very much...

FAN 1. No thank YOU! And you Mr Seagoon!

(He leaves.)

SECOMBE. We're going to get a lot of this – I hope! It's a success Spike, you're just going to have to bloody well admit it.

(Another **FAN** *accosts him.)*

FAN 2. The wife and I came to the recording… You're incredibly funny… go on tell me a joke.

SPIKE. No.

FAN 2. But you're a comedian.

SPIKE. What do you do for a living?

FAN 2. I'm a carpenter.

SPIKE. OK, make me a table.

(They laugh… but unsure if he's joking.)

SECOMBE. Thank you. Lovely of you to come.

SPIKE. I could use that…

*(**SPIKE** scribbles his bon mot down on a fag packet.)*

SECOMBE. You know your trouble is you work too hard. You should relax more. You don't have to go round with a sign that says 'I am funny'.

SPIKE. I just don't have your and Peter's confidence. You can sing…

SECOMBE. I'm a Bel Canto… or rather a Can Belto

SPIKE. *(Not really listening.)* …and Peter can do all those voices…

SECOMBE. Yes. The only voice he can't do is Peter Sellers. You've got a voice of your own.

SPIKE. *(Not really listening.)* But Peter has the advantage of coming from a showbiz background…

SECOMBE. I thought your mum and dad were on the stage?

SPIKE. It was the stage of the Bombay Palace of Varieties singing 'The Road to Mandalay' out of tune. It wasn't exactly headlining at the Palladium.

SECOMBE. The trouble with you Spike, is that you worry too much.

SPIKE. I know. It's a source of constant worry.

> (**SECOMBE** *rolls his eyes wearily as* **SPIKE** *scribbles the joke down on back of napkin.*)

SPIKE. Why can't I be like you? You've got Myra. You're solid as a rock. I'm still all over the place.

SECOMBE. I didn't have it as bad as you. I was just a bit battle weary. You had your brains bombed out.

SPIKE. I just can't help feeling so angry all the time.

SECOMBE. Who with?

SPIKE. Everyone. The Army. The BBC. Everyone my dad had to call 'Sir'.

SECOMBE. Your father is a difficult man...

SPIKE. I inherited two things from my father. Emotional instability and piles.

> (**SECOMBE** *laughs.*)

I've no idea what a normal marriage looks like. My father's favourite hobby was dressing up as a cowboy...

> (*Flashback. We hear Western music, and* **SPIKE**'s *father* **LEO** *appears, wearing a full cowboy outfit, including chaps.*)

LEO. Reach for the sky!

> ((**YOUNG**) **SPIKE** *puts his hands up.*)

This town ain't big enough for the two of us.

YOUNG SPIKE. Catford?

> (**SPIKE'S MUM** *appears dressed as a cowgirl with tray of very English tea and biscuits.*)

MOTHER. Your tea's ready!

LEO. Mighty grateful ma'am!

> (**LEO** *takes his Stetson off, and with it comes his black wig. He hastily puts the wig back on. Back to* **SPIKE** *and* **SECOMBE** *in the pub.*)

SPIKE. I mean, is that... normal?

SECOMBE. *(Chuckling.)* No, but at least it's not boring. Your dad is unconventional... a bit of a rebel. He doesn't like authority much, does he?

SPIKE. He doesn't like **anyone** much. Anyone who isn't Irish. Anyone who **is** Irish...

SECOMBE. What about the Welsh?

SPIKE. Don't even go there! All that chapel and Eisteddfodds and Land of my Fathers...

SECOMBE. *(Begins singing* **[LAND OF MY FATHERS]**, *properly, in Welsh.*)
MAE HEN WLAD FY NHADAU YN ANNWYL I MI,
GWLAD BEIRDD A CHANTORION, ENWOGION O FRI ...

SPIKE. No! Not Welsh! Don't sing! I surrender! I'll come quietly, but only if you will!

> (**SECOMBE** *laughs. Pause. The serious conversation resumes.*)

SECOMBE. You must have learned SOMETHING from your father?

SPIKE. All my father taught me was that the world's run by idiots.

SECOMBE. He's right. But **you** make everyone laugh at them. That's your gift.

SPIKE. Is it? I keep thinking I'm going to die penniless and be buried in a pauper's grave, never getting the any recognition in my lifetime...

SECOMBE. You're good Spike, but you're not bloody Mozart.

(**SPIKE** *laughs.*)

There's nothing wrong with you boyo that can't be sorted out by the love of a good woman.

SPIKE. Or in Peter's case, lots of women.

SECOMBE. So cruel, so true! But at least Peter has someone who unconditionally adores him.

SPIKE. Himself.

(**SECOMBE** *laughs but he's being serious, even if* **SPIKE** *isn't.*)

SECOMBE. You need to share the burden. Find someone Spike.

(*A pause, then* **SPIKE** *dips into his pocket and produces confetti, which he throws in the air.*)

Scene Twelve

(Outside register office. As The confetti falls we hear **[HERE COMES THE BRIDE]** *and* **SPIKE** *and* **SECOMBE** *are suddenly joined by* **SELLERS, MAIN-WILSON** *and* **MYRA, SECOMBE**'s *Welsh wife – and* **SPIKE**'s *new bride* **JUNE**.*)*

SECOMBE. It was a lovely ceremony.

SELLERS. Yes. Very short.

SPIKE. And best of all – Secombe's wedding present… he didn't sing!

SECOMBE. Don't speak too soon.

*(***SECOMBE** *launches into a version of* **[BREAD OF HEAVEN]**.*)*

Bride of Heaven… Bride of Heaven…

SPIKE. What's Welsh for stop?

SECOMBE. *(Continues.)* …feed me till I want no more, want no more…

SPIKE. Myra, help me!

MYRA. Harry, you're showing off again!

*(***SECOMBE** *stops immediately.)*

(To **JUNE**.*)* You've got to keep them under control, love.

MAIN-WILSON. *(To* **JUNE**.*)* Good luck with that.

This is all very jolly – how did you two meet?

JUNE. We were introduced by Peter's girlfriend Ann. We went on a double date.

SPIKE. Peter picked me up in his new Jaguar.

(Flashback in car.)

SELLERS. What do you think of her? Isn't she the most beautiful thing you've ever seen?

SPIKE. Yes, Ann's lovely.

SELLERS. I meant the car.

SPIKE. It's a car. You get a new car every week. What was wrong with the old car?

SELLERS. It was facing in the wrong direction.

SPIKE. You change cars more regularly than you change your underwear!

(Back to SPIKE explaining to MAIN-WILSON.)

It was an awkward first date. June was the most beautiful creature I had ever seen. Perhaps It was the light.

JUNE. Perhaps it was the fact that I came to the door dressed only in a bath towel.

SPIKE. I was shy and she was half Italian. For reasons known only to myself, I spent the rest of the evening pretending to be Italian as well.

(Flashback.)

(Nervously puts on Italian accent.) Buon Giorno signora... I too am from Italia...

JUNE. *(Very English.)* Oh yes? Whereabouts?

SPIKE. La bella... Catford.

> *(Dance music starts. Suddenly we are in a nightclub with glitterball. JUNE and SPIKE dance.)*

JUNE. So how long have you been in this country?

SPIKE. Forgive me... I do not speak the linguine... so greatly

JUNE. Ah... That's sweet.

> (**SPIVVY MAN** *approaches, trying to but in.*)

SPIVVY MAN. Fancy a dance darling? You don't want to get stuck with this idiot.

JUNE. Don't be so unkind... he's a very charming person... his English isn't very good, that's all.

SPIKE. No Inglese parliamente!

JUNE. *(To* **SPIKE.***)* Let's go and get a drink...

SPIKE. I'm really sorry, but I can't keep this up.

JUNE. What?

SPIKE. I'm not Italian. I'm a friend of Peter's. I'm a comedian.

JUNE. Well I don't think that's funny at all!

SPIKE. I know, I'm sorry, I started and I just sort of couldn't stop...

JUNE. I think I'd better go.

SPIKE. Please... I just wasn't confident being myself... it's easier to hide behind a stupid character. You're just so beautiful and amazing, and I'm just hopeless...

JUNE. I don't know...

SPIKE. Please. Can we try again, only this time with me as me?

> (**JUNE** *looks unsure.*)

Prego! Prego! Bella... Lugosi!

> (*She laughs. And they kiss. We are back at the wedding.* **SECOMBE** *throws more confetti.*)

SECOMBE. So, you two lovebirds, where's the honeygoon?

JUNE. Four days in beautiful… Bayswater.

MYRA. Just four days?

MAIN-WILSON. That's plenty of time!

SELLERS. More than enough!

JUNE. I know, I know. Spike's got to write the next series.

MYRA. *(To* **JUNE.***)* Congratulations – you're now married to the Goons.

> *(***JUNE** *blows a loud raspberry.)*

Scene Thirteen

(SPIKE's flat. JUNE leads SPIKE to his desk, with the typewriter. Like MAIN-WILSON before, she sits him down, puts paper in the typewriter, places his hands on the keyboard and he starts typing, slowly at first, then increasingly manically, ripping sheets of paper out of the typewriter and scrunching them up, to the sound of a manic Jazz soundtrack.)

(JUNE brings him a coffee. He doesn't acknowledge it.)

JUNE. Can I help?

SPIKE. You read Moriarty.

JUNE. OK.

SPIKE. Moriarty! Moriarty! Where are you?

JUNE/MORIARTY. Here, inside the piano.

SPIKE. What the devil are are you doing in there?

JUNE/MORIARTY. I'm hidin'.

SPIKE. Don't be silly, Haydn's been dead for years…

JUNE. *(Laughs.)* That's funny!

SPIKE. Is it? I'm not sure…

(He screws up paper and starts again.)

JUNE. Do you have to write it **all** yourself?

SPIKE. *(Carrying on typing.)* I've got co-writers but they tend to come up with ideas after the show's ended. It's as if they're trying to drive me insane!

(JUNE laughs.)

I'm not joking. They're bleeding me dry. And half the stuff I write the BBC won't let me do.

JUNE. Why not?

SPIKE. Censorship. They don't like anything that's different or original or takes risks...

> *(On the other side of the stage we see the **BBC EXECUTIVE** sifting through a script with a large red pen striking out out chunks of material.)*

BBC EXECUTIVE. No...

> *(Another page)*

No!

> *(Another page...)*

Definitely no.

> *(Another page...)*

No, sorry

> *(Another page...)*

That's a no-no.

> *(Another page...)*

Nnnnnnooooooo.

> *(Another page...)*

(Laughing at script, then rejecting it...) Yes, it's a 'no'.

> *(Back to **SPIKE** and **JUNE** at the typewriter.)*

JUNE. *(Looking over his shoulder.)* You can't blame them for being a bit careful, though. You've written 'bollocks' there. Obviously they won't allow you to say that.

SPIKE. No – I just write 'bollocks' when I can't think of anything funny to say. I'll fill the line in later.

(**JUNE** *holds up page.*)

JUNE. There's a lot of bollocks here.

SPIKE. Everyone's a critic.

JUNE. When's the deadline?

SPIKE. Yesterday.

(**JUNE** *laughs.*)

That's not a joke either.

JUNE. What can I do to help?

SPIKE. Just be here.

(*She gives him a kiss on his head.*)

JUNE. What are you writing?

SPIKE. A Rewrite of Series 2, Episode 7.

(**JUNE** *puts plate of sandwiches by the typewriter. He doesn't even look up.* **SPIKE** *continues typing manically.*)

Or it might be a rewrite of a rewrite of Series 3, Episode 12.

JUNE. Please come to bed.

(**SPIKE** *continues typing manically.*)

SPIKE. It's no good. I've got to do the whole thing again.

JUNE. Who says?

SPIKE. Me!

JUNE. You need to sleep.

SPIKE. I don't have time for sleep. The bloody BBC's seen to that! And bloody Sellers.

JUNE. I thought you said he didn't write anything anyway?

SPIKE. You don't understand! Already my wife doesn't understand me!

> (*Bangs his head against the typewriter.* **JUNE** *is in tears. She doesn't know what to do or how to deal with him.* **SPIKE** *realises this, and tearfully hugs her.*)

I'm sorry love. Cheer up. It could be worse.

JUNE. How?

SPIKE. At least we don't have a baby to worry about.

> (*We hear a* **BABY**'s *cry.*)

BABY. Waaaah!!!!!

> (**SPIKE** *reacts with alarm. The cry gets louder and louder.*)

SPIKE. Sorry, June, I've got to go…

JUNE. Why?

SPIKE. The BBC …

> (*He sleepwalks from his desk straight into the BBC Office.*)

Scene Fourteen

(BBC Office. It's a programme review with **BBC EXECUTIVE, SPIKE** *and* **MAIN-WILSON.** *They are listening to a* Goon Show *recording on a large old-fashioned tape recorder.)*

BBC EXECUTIVE. What I'm saying is that this is not acceptable...

(He presses a button. Nothing happens. Presses another button and the tape fast forwards, we hear speeded up voices. Then very slow. Then stops.)

MAIN-WILSON. Would you like Janet to work it?

*(***JANET** *the programme assistant enters.)*

BBC EXECUTIVE. If you'd be so kind, this technology changing all the time, it's jolly difficult to keep up. When shows were recorded on gramophone records, it was all a lot easier.

*(***JANET** *easily sorts the problem, pressing one button. We hear a* Goon Show *with* **SELLERS** *sounding exactly like the Queen and a commentator sounding like Richard Dimbleby.)*

DINGLEBEE. This is me, Richard Dinglebee speaking to you on the Great Golden Microphone of State... and here comes the guest of honour the Duchess Boil de Spudswell...

(Sound effects cheers. Band plays **[RULE BRITANNIA]** *badly.)*

SPUDSWELL. It is my privilege and provelege to declare this building open, and gawd bless all who sail in her...

BBC EXECUTIVE. Stop it there miss... er Janet.

> (**JANET** *stops the tape.*)

It is quite clear that this Duchess Boil de Spudswell is none other than Her Majesty the Queen.

SPIKE. No, no, it's the Duchess Boil de Spudswell.

BBC EXECUTIVE. I'm not an idiot, you know Mr Milligan.

SPIKE. No, I didn't know that.

BBC EXECUTIVE. I know, for example, that you continually try to smuggle filthy jokes into the script. A pink oboe indeed! It's pretty poor stuff.

> (**SPIKE** *tries to look innocent, shaking his head barely concealing a smirk.*)

I also know that the milk you all drink during recordings is actually laced with brandy.

SPIKE. Is it? I thought the show was going well!

BBC EXECUTIVE. We cannot have you getting tipsy and lampooning the sovereign on national radio. The BBC has a royal charter, you know. **And** you've been doing the same to Mr Churchill pointing out that his initials are WC.

SPIKE. Well that's because they are. Winston Churchill – WC.

BBC EXECUTIVE. There is no excuse for a lavatorial inference. Mr Churchill won the war!

SPIKE. I thought he had some help from one or two of us.

BBC EXECUTIVE. It's still unacceptable. It's like your character Major Bloodnock. Every time he appears he's either surrendering, embezzling money or singing **[DEUTSCHLAND ÜBER ALLES]**.

SPIKE. Good jokes.

BBC EXECUTIVE. Which all seem to be aimed at the officer class.

MAIN-WILSON. I don't think that's fair...

BBC EXECUTIVE. Nor do I! It's very **un**fair. A lot of people think your take on the war is very disrespectful to the survivors.

SPIKE. I **am** a survivor. **All** of us in the Goons are survivors.

> *(Suddenly we are a bombardment of explosions and smoke fills the stage. We are back in Monte Cassino.)*

Scene Fifteen

(Monte Cassino. We hear an explosion, and through the smoke we see **SPIKE** *staggering dazed down the hill. His leg is bleeding, but he's oblivious as he stumbles back down towards the command post.)*

MAJOR JENKINS. You're going the wrong bloody way Milligan!

SPIKE. *(Can't hear him.)* I can't hear you.

MAJOR JENKINS. *(Bellowing.)* What's the matter with you? Are you a coward?

SPIKE. *(Stammering.)* W-w-we were... I-I-I was...

MAJOR JENKINS. Get back up the bloody hill and do your job!

(A **SERGEANT** *intervenes.)*

SERGEANT. He's been hit sir.

MAJOR JENKINS. Idiot!

SERGEANT. I'll deal with him sir.

*(***MAJOR*** ducks and runs off.)*

Come with me, Milligan...

*(***SPIKE*** is about to stumble off the hillside in the other direction.)*

Where are you going?

SPIKE. *(Grins, dazed.)* Can we have the next dance over the precipice, darling?

SERGEANT. Are you all right?

*(**SPIKE** is dazed and terrified. He screws himself up into a foetal ball. **JUNE** enters. He's back at home.)*

Scene Sixteen

(**SPIKE**'s *flat.* **SPIKE** *is sitting on the floor.* **JUNE** *joins him.*)

JUNE. It's all right love. It's just a dream. You're not there.

(**SPIKE** *wakes up in a sweat.*)

(*He lights a cigarette.*)

SPIKE. It's always the same. I'm so tired I can't even have an original nightmare!

JUNE. Try to get some sleep. It's gone three.

SPIKE. You know what was good about the army?

JUNE. That it gave you nightmares?

SPIKE. (*Ignoring her.*) What was good about the army was that everything was done for you.

JUNE. So just like being married.

SPIKE. It was all so easy back then. I didn't have any responsibilities, didn't have any debts, didn't have a mortgage… it was a great life in the army – when you weren't being killed.

JUNE. Spike, stop worrying, we're fine…

SPIKE. In the army you could be funny for fun. It wasn't work. There was no pressure.

JUNE. Get some sleep. Or at least let me get some.

SPIKE. Yes. I am going to sleep right now, as ordered. By the right, drift… off!

(*Pause.* **SPIKE** *suddenly sits up.*)

Can you hear that?

JUNE. I can't hear anything.

SPIKE. Music.

JUNE. There's nothing.

SPIKE. *(Shouts.)* Stop that bloody music!

> *(This wakes the baby, who starts crying. They are both now wide awake.* **JUNE** *gets up.)*

Don't leave me!

JUNE. I'm not leaving you. Its Laura…

SPIKE. Everyone leaves me. My parents left me.

JUNE. They emigrated to Australia.

SPIKE. Its a long way to go to avoid me.

JUNE. Who else has left you?

SPIKE. Bentine left me.

JUNE. You told me you were glad to see the back of him

SPIKE. I preferred the front of him.

JUNE. Who else?

SPIKE. Denis is leaving.

JUNE. Producer Denis?

SPIKE. He's buggering off to work for Tony Hancock.

JUNE. Oh he's funny.

SPIKE. I know – that's the whole bloody problem. Denis clearly thinks he's funnier than we are.

JUNE. He's just the producer. You said a monkey could produce the show.

SPIKE. Will you please stop proving what an idiot I am. This is a disaster. It's the beginning of the end.

JUNE. I have to go. But only next door.

SPIKE. Without Denis in charge Sellers will be out of control, demanding more rewrites while sodding off at every opportunity to do his bloody films and buy more bloody cars and saying why should he stick around and watch Milligan going mad why can't he be a dull bastard like myself! But Sellers is as mad as I am maybe madder with his bloody superstitions and clairvoyants and his spirit guiding his career and telling him he used to be Napoleon or Caesar or Leonardo Da Vinci in a previous life, funny how he was never anyone ordinary... but with Denis gone he'll be insufferable and I'll be working myself into the grave just to make Peter fucking Sellers famous...

*(Suddenly, **SPIKE** has an epiphany.)*

That's it!

JUNE. *(Offstage.)* What is it?

SPIKE. I know what I have to do!

*(**SPIKE** leaps up and rummages through a (kitchen) drawer. A bleary **JUNE** appears at the door with the baby.)*

JUNE. What are you doing?

SPIKE. I'm fixing everything! I'm going to make it stop!

JUNE. What? How?

SPIKE. Simple! I'm going to kill Peter Sellers!

(Wearing only his pyjamas, he grabs a coat and strides out of door.)

Scene Seventeen

*(**SELLERS**' flat. **SELLERS** is listening to the 1812 overture and is wearing a Napoleon hat in his dressing gown, with his arm across his chest and his hand tucked into his dressing gown.)*

(We hear banging on the door. He hastily removes the hat.)

SPIKE. Let me in!

SELLERS. *(Offstage.)* What?

SPIKE. Let me in! Let me in now!

SELLERS. Spike?

SPIKE. Open up! I've come to kill Peter Sellers!

*(**SELLERS** emerges groggily.)*

SELLERS. For God's sake Spike, do you know what time it is?

SPIKE. Time to end it all.

SELLERS. What 'all'?

SPIKE. You've been driving me mad...

SELLERS. We have our differences from time to time but we always sort it out over a drink or two...

SPIKE. What about the music?

SELLERS. I don't know what you're talking about.

SPIKE. The music you've been secretly piping into my flat night and day... keeping me awake... stopping me writing...

SELLERS. Why would I want to stop you writing?

SPIKE. I know you're out to get me!

SELLERS. I'm out to get you to finish the script, that's all.

SPIKE. I'm sorry it has to end like this...

SELLERS. Is this a prank?

> (**SPIKE** *smashes through the door. The sound of a siren can be heard, getting closer. In the background a blue flashing light.*)

What the hell are you doing?

SPIKE. I feel like my head's going to burst wide open!

SELLERS. Come on Spike, this isn't funny any more. Go home before I call the police.

SPIKE. You don't understand I can't take it any more! I have to stop this madness – and there's only one way!

> (*He pulls out his weapon and brandishes it. It looks like a knife, but isn't. It's a potato peeler.* **SELLERS** *clocks this.*)

SELLERS. Spike, that's a potato peeler. What are you going to do – peel me?

End of Act One

ACT TWO

Scene One

(Radio Studio. **JANET** *stands at her sound effects table. We see the same sound effects, now including a trombone, a hubbly bubbly pipe, a large cabbage and a cleaver.)*

JANET. Though some in the BBC Sound Effects Department undoubtedly find Mr Milligan to be something of a nuisance, there is no doubt that he has accelerated innovation within the department. When performing live, the spot effects operator will still use ordinary objects. So, for example, in historical sketches any guillotining requirements can be met by a trusty cabbage and cleaver...

(She demonstrates with the cabbage.)

...while the slide whistle remains a staple for reproducing the effect of someone falling off a cliff...

(She demonstrates blowing into a swanee whistle.)

And jumping back up again.

(She demonstrates blowing into a swanee whistle in reverse.)

However, as magnetic tape has come to replace gramophone records – forgive me if I'm getting too technical – new technology has allowed greater inventiveness and flexibility for all of us working on the Goon Show. So whereas once we would have produced a sound effect like Major Bloodnock's stomach after eating curried eggs, like so...

(She blows a trombone.)

Now, we can mix various effects elements on tape to create a more sophisticated and complex audio Goonscape, achieved here by overlaying burps, whoops from oscillators, water splashes, corklike pops, and light artillery blasts.

(She switches on a tape which plays a vulgar bubbly farty noise followed by an explosion.)

The sound of the future. Something of a breakthrough for radio audiophonics. One of our sound effects has become rather famous – something of a celebrity with its own fan club. It is of course Fred the Oyster, who first appeared in the show entitled The Sinking of Westminster Pier.

(She plays the tape recorder again. We hear the strange gurgling, braying sound effect.)

A combination of tape recorded donkeys braying, deflating balloons and a recording of Mr Secombe blowing a raspberry at slow speed.

(She turns the tape recorder off.)

With all these galloping advances in sound technology, there **are** still complaints... but not from Spike.

*(Enter **SPIKE**, bounding in and kissing **JANET**.)*

SPIKE. That is brilliant! That sounds **exactly** like a giant oyster being opened up by the oyster sexers to determine if Fred's a boy or a girl!

(*Enter* **BBC EXECUTIVE**.)

BBC EXECUTIVE. I'm afraid I found it very coarse. And Mildred's never liked oysters, after the incident in the restaurant at Whitstable.

JANET. (*To* **SPIKE**.) I've been working on that other effect you wanted for Sunday's show…

(**JANET** *plays the tape recorder. We hear the effect of a high-speed merry-go-round combined with motor engine.*)

BBC EXECUTIVE. What's that?

SPIKE. That is the sound of a Wurlitzer being driven through the desert at breakneck speed. By a man with a broken neck.

BBC EXECUTIVE. It sounds to me like a lot of time and money for a single not-very-good joke, and a rather extravagant waste of the one pound licence fee!

JANET. Not all the effects are complicated. Look at this.

(*She holds up a bulging sock.*)

BBC EXECUTIVE. And what's that?

SPIKE. It's a sock full of custard.

BBC EXECUTIVE. And what's it meant to sound like?

SPIKE. A sock full of custard.

(**SPIKE** *hits the* **BBC EXECUTIVE** *with it. There is a loud squelch.*)

It's uncanny!

BBC EXECUTIVE. Sometimes you overstep the mark, Mr Milligan.

SPIKE. You're very kind.

BBC EXECUTIVE. I gather **you're** not very well? We all heard about the unfortunate incident with Mr Sellers.

SPIKE. It was a joke. No-one here ever understands my jokes!

BBC EXECUTIVE. Yes, I've always found it a problem.

SPIKE. No wonder I'm depressed.

BBC EXECUTIVE. Why don't you take some time off? This afternoon perhaps? We don't want a repeat of the attempted potato peeler homicide.

SPIKE. Nobody got hurt. Not even a potato.

BBC EXECUTIVE. We really can't have writers going around threatening the lives of the talent. It just won't do. And it's embarrassing for the BBC to have one of its employees ending up in a strait jacket.

SPIKE. It didn't suit me. I didn't like the cut. Terrible tailor.

BBC EXECUTIVE. I'm serious, Milligan.

SPIKE. I know. You're the Head of Comedy.

Scene Two

(Rehearsal room. Jazz music as the scene changes. We are back in the Radio Theatre with the team reading from scripts.)

SECOMBE /SEAGOON. So let me get this right. Neddie Seagoon is swimming along under water when he comes across an oyster.

SELLERS. As you do...

JANET. I thought the higher uppers didn't like the oyster material.

SPIKE. That's why we're going to do more of it!

SECOMBE/SEAGOON. So Knock knock knockety knock

(JANET produces a door creaking sound.)

Hello young lady

SELLERS. *(As a very old woman.)* What do you want?

SECOMBE/SEAGOON. Are you Pearl?

SELLERS. No, I'm her mother.

SECOMBE/SEAGOON. Ah, mother of pearl!

(SPIKE falls off chair laughing.)

SELLERS. We regret to announce the death of that joke.

(He pretends to play the **[LAST POST]** *on imaginary bugle.)*

A tragic end. And the beginning wasn't much better.

SPIKE. That won't stop me using it!

(Voice off on tannoy.)

ETON. Well I thought it was brilliant! And brilliantly performed.

SECOMBE. Who is this amazingly perceptive personage?

> *(Enter* **PETER ETON.** *A moustachioed, jolly, blazer-wearing type. He has a pronounced limp.)*

ETON. Did no-one tell you? I'm your new producer. Peter Eton. I'm replacing Denis.

SECOMBE. Goon but not forgotten.

SPIKE. Whoever he was.

ETON. I've been transferred from the drama department.

SELLERS. So what do you know about comedy?

ETON. Well I **was** in the Navy.

> *(They all laugh despite themselves.)*

SECOMBE. *(Sings.)*
ALL THE NICE GIRLS LOVE A SAILOR,
ALL THE NICE GIRLS LOVE A TAR ...

> *(The others join in this old* **[MUSIC HALL SONG]**.*)*

SECOMBE, MILLIGAN & SELLERS.
... FOR THERE'S SOMETHING ABOUT A SAILOR,
WELL YOU KNOW WHAT SAILORS ARE ...

> *(They dance around him flirtatiously.)*

ETON. This sailor does have some thoughts about how we might improve the comedy...

SELLERS. Says the man from drama!

SPIKE. So we wear tights, do it in verse and call it Hamlet?

ETON. Not a bad idea. Have you seen Shakespeare's audience figures? And he gets a lot of repeats.

(They laugh.)

It goes without saying that I love the show and I'm incredibly excited about working with you all.

SELLERS. But you love it so much you want to change it.

ETON. What I'm saying is it could be even better. The best.

SECOMBE. So what are these 'thoughts' of yours?

ETON. I was thinking we should look at the structure of the shows... maybe consider it in terms of a three act play rather than just random sketches. Tell one story all the way through...

SPIKE. I like that idea – we take everything to its illogical conclusion.

ETON. I think with a solid plot we can create a believable Goon world. And the music's taking up nearly half the show and interferes with the storyline, so we're going to cut it right down.

SPIKE. That means I'm going to have to write twice as much!

ETON. Which means that the show will be twice as enjoyable.

SPIKE. For you maybe!

ETON. Then we put Harry centre stage as a sort of leading man...

SPIKE. ...albeit a small blubbery welsh blob of a leading man...

ETON. ...and we'll have a full half-hour yarn which will engage the audience in a coherent narrative while allowing room for more of Peter's voices and improvisations.

SELLERS. *(Adopts German accent.)* Mein Führer you are einer Vundershurn Gerhimmler! I vill follow your orders to ze ends of ze earth!

> *(**SELLERS** clicks his heels and salutes.)*

SPIKE. It all sounds suspiciously like drama to me. And you haven't mentioned jokes.

ETON. I'm also going to insist on proper rehearsals.

SPIKE. At last! A joke!

> *(They laugh.)*

ETON. Of course the jokes are paramount but this way the jokes become less random... and we can really go to town on the sound effects – which are just as important as the spoken word.

SPIKE. This man is a genius!

SECOMBE. Or rather a Goonius!

ETON. And every episode should have a clear identity as a spoof adventure... like I don't know, The Ascent of Mount Everest, or The Building of the Suez Canal... or... 50,000 Leagues Under the Sea...

> *(**JANET** blows through straw into a glass of water for a bubbling noise.)*
>
> *(Note: She proceeds to illustrate the titles with sound effects performed in quick succession so as not to impede the flow of titles.)*

SELLERS. ... Britain's First Atomic Cannon...

> *(**JANET** fires pop-gun.)*

SECOMBE. ...the dreaded Batter Pudding Hurler of Bexhill on Sea...

> *(**JANET** makes squelch with a plunger and a bucket of goop.)*

SPIKE. ...Through the Sound Barrier in an Airing Cupboard...

> (**JANET** *creates a whoosh sound waving a tube of air.*)

ETON. Now we are getting somewhere.

> (**JANET** *beams.*)

SPIKE. Give this man a medal!

> (**SPIKE** *puts his teaspoon in* **ETON**'s *top pocket so that it looks like a medal.*)

Now, since we are all getting on so well I've got some ideas of my own.

ETON. Fire away!

SPIKE. One: I'd like some more money! Two: More money please. And three – did I mention the money?

Scene Three

(Photo shoot. Up-beat jazz music plays as we move into a photo shoot. The Goons go through an array of comic poses as flashbulbs pop and the Goons are interviewed by a posh **FEMALE REPORTER**. *They're pulling faces, posing with comedy props.* **SPIKE** *blows the trumpet the wrong way, puts it on* **SECOMBE***'s head, while* **SECOMBE** *is smoking a leek like a cigar.* **SELLERS** *wears a pith helmet and is armed with a blunderbus.)*

FEMALE REPORTER. There's a huge worldwide following for your anarchic brand of comedy... can you tell the readers of the *Radio Times* how on earth do you keep the standards so high?

SECOMBE. Brandy and more brandy.

FEMALE REPORTER. And with all that you have achieved where do you go from here?

SECOMBE. The pub!

FEMALE REPORTER. You are so madcap! I mean, some people say you're the funniest show since 'ITMA'

SELLERS. *(As an exaggerated Noël Coward.)* My dear you are not only the most intelligent journalist I have ever met, but also the most delightful... you have extraordinary eyes like limpid pools, which I want to jump into and drown myself in your utter loveliness...

SPIKE. What Peter's saying is that it's tough... it's very difficult to maintain the quality, and the expectation is increasingly high and you live in continual fear that you'll disappoint everyone, and you never get any encouragement from the BBC...

(Everyone is a bit embarrassed by **SPIKE***'s mood-dampening misery.)*

SECOMBE. Needle nardle noo!

FEMALE REPORTER. It must be such fun working together.

SECOMBE & SELLERS. Yes!

SPIKE. *(Simultaneously.)* No!

Scene Four

> (**SPIKE** *leaves the photoshoot and moves to the other side of the stage with his typewriter and a vast pile of fresh paper waiting to be filled with words. He begins to type furiously with the* **[FLIGHT OF THE BUMBLEBEE]** *playing and him singing along as before but this time the music begins to slow as does his rate of typing until he comes to a halt and stares into space. He is exhausted. At the same time we see* **JUNE**, **MYRA** *and* **SECOMBE** *waiting for* **SPIKE** *to come down for dinner.*)

JUNE. I'm sorry about Spike. I'm sure he'll be down soon.

SECOMBE. *(To* **JUNE**.*)* It's all right. It's difficult being married to a comic genius.

MYRA. I wouldn't know, would I?

SECOMBE. Oh you Jezebel!

> (**MYRA** *laughs, flicking a napkin at him.*)

> (**JUNE** *calls up to* **SPIKE**.)

JUNE. Spike! The food's getting cold!

> (**SPIKE** *doesn't respond.*)

I'm so embarrassed. I don't know what to do.

MYRA. Don't worry. We're having a lovely time down here. The dinner is delicious. And Harry will eat everything, you can be sure of that.

SECOMBE. I have to – I have to keep my trousers full!

> (*We go back to* **SPIKE** *bashing away at the typewriter.*)

(On the other side of the stage **MYRA** *and* **SECOMBE** *are leaving.* **JUNE** *is helping them on with their coats.)*

MYRA. It's important to keep them grounded. When Harry gets too big for his boots I make him take the bins out.

SECOMBE. I'm a has-bin!

*(**MYRA** laughs.)*

MYRA. Oh yes – and laugh at all his jokes! Whatever he says.

SECOMBE. I love you too darling.

MYRA. *(Laughing.)* Hilarious, boyo! Really, it's like dealing with children.

SECOMBE. *(Serious.)* And you know, June, we are always here for you.

JUNE. Unlike Spike.

(They leave. **JUNE** *Crosses to* **SPIKE**.*)*

The guests have gone.

SPIKE. I was about to come down.

JUNE. It's one o'clock in the morning.

SPIKE. I'm sorry I just couldn't stop... did I miss anything important?

JUNE. Yes. We talked about who should take the bins out.

SPIKE. *(Testily.)* If you want me to do all the domestic chores as well as write thirty episodes of a new series, then fine. I'll do it. Just say.

*(**JUNE** throws scrunched up paper at him.)*

JUNE. Myra said the best way to deal with a comedian is to laugh at everything he says. I must say I am finding it difficult. Even when you do say something. But most of the time you're up here working in silence.

> (**SPIKE** *doesn't respond.*)

I said '**most of the time you're up here working in silence**'.

SPIKE. Read the sign on the door.

JUNE. *(Reads.)* 'Do not disturb. Disturbed enough already.'

> *(He continues to bash away at the typewriter. We switch to a Goon rehearsal.)*

Scene Five

(Radio Studio. Another Goons rehearsal. **SECOMBE, SELLERS,** *all at the microphone.* **MILLIGAN** *is absent.)*

SELLERS. Peter, I thought you said we were having **proper** rehearsals? Where's bloody Spike?

ETON. We'll start anyway. Go from the top.

SECOMBE. *(Reading from script.)* It is I Sir Hilary Seagoon leading the British Expedition to climb the highest mountain in the world. But first… we have to **build** it.

> *(***SPIKE** *rushes in. He's in disarray, and goes straight onto the stage microphone.)*

SPIKE. *(In gruff voice.)* Hullo…

SECOMBE. *(Surprised, and beginning to crack up.)* Who are you supposed to be?

MILLIGAN. I'm a husky.

> *(***PETER ETON** *appears, annoyed as* **SECOMBE** *corpses.)*

ETON. No! No! No! What's going on?

SPIKE. It's a new voice.

ETON. We don't need any new voices. It's not in the script.

SPIKE. I thought it was funny.

ETON. What we've got is funny! We don't need ad libs. Ad libs mean we run over time, which means more editing. What we need is to keep to the plan. What we need is some discipline.

SPIKE. It's like being back in the bloody military!

ETON. Yes! It is! Sometimes it's the only way to get things done! And it stops everything becoming a bloody shambles.

SPIKE. Like the war!

ETON. You're not the only one who was in it Spike! You're not the only one who's seen action! I was invalided out after Dunkirk! Denis Main-Wilson was one of the first men on the Normandy beaches. But we don't all use it as an excuse for doing whatever the hell we like!

> *(Pause. Everyone is a bit stunned by this outburst.)*

That said, I'm completely wrong, it's a very funny ad-lib. And it's now in the script. Sorry, but that's an order.

> *(Other Goons give **ETON** a round of applause.)*

I am sympathetic Spike, but try to remember, the war **is** over!

SPIKE. But **not** the war with the BBC!

> *(**ETON** walks out of recording studio...)*

Scene Six

(... Into **BBC EXECUTIVE***'s Office.* **BBC EXECUTIVE** *is talking to man with ventriloquist dummy. It is* **PETER BROUGH** *and his puppet* **ARCHIE***.)*

ETON. You wanted to see me?

BBC EXECUTIVE. Yes come in... you know Peter Brough and of course Archie.

ARCHIE. Good gorning.

ETON. Good morning.

BBC EXECUTIVE. The thing is that management had a bit of a brainstorm and thought we could combine the established star power of Educating Archie with the madcap foolery of the Goons. Sort of Educating Goonie.

ARCHIE. Grilliant!

ETON. I agree its grilliant, but I am not sure Spike is going to see it like that. And he has been quite critical of Archie in the past...

ARCHIE. Gloody gastard! He can just gugger off!

BBC EXECUTIVE. I don't think this is particularly helpful so I think we will leave it on the back burner for now and see how it develops.

> *(***PETER BROUGH** *gets up and leaves the room with* **ARCHIE***.)*

Thanks for coming in Mr. Brough and of course Archie!

ARCHIE. Gye Gye!

> *(***BROUGH** *exits, muttering to his puppet.)*

BBC EXECUTIVE. Pity. Maybe its an idea ahead of its time, mashing up two completely different programmes and seeing what happens...

ETON. It's the fate of visionaries to be ignored in their own time...

BBC EXECUTIVE. I DO think the Goons need something to get them back on track...

ETON. But the show is going really well...

BBC EXECUTIVE. But is it? You see some of us think it's in danger of being submerged by its own gusto and extreme eccentricity. I have the feeling lately that the cast have got somewhat out of control at the microphone. If these tendencies are not arrested very quickly the show may well collapse like one of Mildred's souffles.

ETON. For god's sake don't say that to them. This bunch of neurotics need all the encouragement they can get.

BBC EXECUTIVE. The problem, as always, is Milligan.

I understand that he generally goes to pieces if faced with too much to do. Hence the ahem... Sellers incident...

ETON. In the light of his problems, he has made a request to postpone the show for a few weeks.

BBC EXECUTIVE. *(Horrified.)* We can't have that! Postponing the show? That would leave the general public wanting. The show is at the height of its popularity, however baffling that might seem to some of us. However, we must consider the millions of listeners who get so much enjoyment out of *The Goons*, and who might write to the newspapers to complain about BBC management if there were to be a hole in the schedules.

ETON. That's very considerate of you. The audience must come first. But you could improve morale by other means.

BBC EXECUTIVE. How so?

ETON. Can't you do anything about the money?

BBC EXECUTIVE. Oh here we go! It's always about money!

ETON. The fact is that Sellers gets thirty six pounds and fifteen shillings an episode. Secombe gets thirty one pounds eighteen shillings. Spike, meanwhile, gets the princely sum of eighteen pounds and eighteen shillings.

BBC EXECUTIVE. It does seem a lot. Are you saying we should pay him **less**?

ETON. No, I'm saying you're paying the man who writes it all **half** as much as you pay the others!

BBC EXECUTIVE. But they're the talent!

ETON. I know at his worst Spike is a petulant schoolboy with an almost pathological distrust of authority...

BBC EXECUTIVE. Yes.

ETON. But at his best he is a near genius.

BBC EXECUTIVE. Is he? You see I recently had an exchange of letters with him regarding scheduling and to be frank with you I wasn't at all impressed.

> (*We see* **SPIKE** *at side of stage reading out letter.*)

SPIKE. Dear Sir,

Regarding your letter advising the change of time for *The Goon Show* to mid Sunday Afternoon may I point out that although I am available at this time anyone who comes to hear a show at three forty five p.m. on a Sunday afternoon must be a) Without a home and b) Gormless. Yours sincerely Spike Milligan.

*(We then see **BBC EXECUTIVE** reading his letter in return.)*

BBC EXECUTIVE. Dear Mr. Milligan, regarding your letter of the twenty second of September, may I point out that it would surely have been much better to have said Homeless rather than Without a home as 'Homeless' goes much better with 'Gormless'. Maybe **you** should manage the department and **I** should write the scripts? Yours sincerely etc, etc.

*(**SPIKE** increasingly annoyed.)*

SPIKE. Psychologically, three forty five p.m. on a Sunday afternoon is a bad time to perform a comedy show. It is like doing Rigoletto in the middle of Bond Street.

*(**BBC EXECUTIVE** responds.)*

BBC EXECUTIVE. For your information you spelt 'psychologically' incorrectly. And we are in fact so desperately short of studios now that I think it more than likely that our next production will indeed be performed in the middle of Bond Street.

(To himself.)

A rather amusing riposte methought.

SPIKE. All right you win. But please keep my name in mind for tickets for Rigoletto when it is performed on Bond Street.

BBC EXECUTIVE. *(Getting more pompous.)* From the Executive Head of Comedy and Variety, bracket, productions. Reference CFM slash O3 slash V. Dear Mr Milligan, it has been reported to me that despite constant requests for early delivery, your scripts for the Goon product continue to arrive late. This causes considerable last-minute work for the production team. I must ask you to deliver scripts no later than Thursday.

SPIKE. Dear Executive Head of Comedy and variety, bracket, productions. Reference CFM slash O3 slash V. I'm afraid I can't deliver the script on time because I'm too busy writing letters to you. Reference FU C slash K O FF!

Scene Seven

> (*Outside* **SPIKE**'s *office door. We hear manic typing.* **JUNE** *enters, carrying a tray of food. The door is now locked, and* **SPIKE** *won't answer. She leaves the tray outside the door. She meets* **PETER ETON**.)

JUNE. I'm sorry Peter, he doesn't want to see anyone.

ETON. How do you know?

JUNE. There's a sign on the door that says 'Go Away'.

ETON. The thing is, we don't have a script. And he hasn't been into the office for days.

JUNE. I know. I don't know what to do. It's getting worse. And nothing I do seems to help.

I don't know what he wants… he's only happy when he's working but then the work's making him unhappy.

ETON. I know Spike thinks we're putting him under intolerable pressure but if you're a comedy writer that's the job. Galton and Simpson are writing just as many Hancock shows a year if not **more**.

JUNE. The person who's putting **real** pressure on him is himself.

> (**ETON** *tries to mollify* **SPIKE** *through the locked door.*)

ETON. It's me, Peter. I know you're upset with me but I've had a word with the Head of Entertainment Variety and he promised to look into the schedule situation. Can you hear me Spike?

SPIKE. No! Go away.

ETON. We've tried to arrange everything around you but we do need you to come into the studio, with something for the others to say. And Peter needs a bit of time to work on the voices...

SPIKE. Peter Sellers is an ungrateful bastard!

ETON. Spike, if you don't open the door the BBC **will** cancel the show. The audience may love it but the powers that be are looking for any excuse to drop it and there'll be nothing I can do to stop them...

> *(The door opens. A very dishevelled* **SPIKE** *hands* **ETON** *script.)*

SPIKE. It needs another draft.

ETON. There isn't time.

SPIKE. You're right. I have been sent to Coventry.

ETON. By your wife?

SPIKE. No – by my management.

> *(***SPIKE** *hastily dons a bow tie and jacket and grabs his trumpet from offstage. A spangly curtain descends and suddenly we are in the Coventry Hippodrome.)*

Scene Eight

(A **MIDLANDS ANNOUNCER** *comes on stage into the spotlight.)*

MIDLANDS ANNOUNCER. Welcome to the Coventry Hippodrome where we are delighted to welcome live on stage the stars of BBC radio, the world famous Goons!

(He applauds but no-one else does.)

So please put your hands together for Mr. Spike Milligan.

*(***SPIKE*** enters.)*

SPIKE. Tonight is NOT the 104th anniversary of the Death of Chopin, so to celebrate that occasion I thought I would play one of his etudes. Then I thought why should I? He never plays any of mine.

(He looks disappointed at the reaction. Starts playing his trumpet. He plays well but breaks off.)

You don't like that one? OK here's another number. Six.

(There is no reaction.)

*(***SECOMBE*** and **SELLERS** *stand to one side watching* **SPIKE** *dying on stage, with his trumpet.)*

OK, so you don't like that number. Here's another one. Thirty seven!

(Audience no reaction.)

(Increasingly desperate.) Forty two... eleven... ninety three... It's called a joke. The trouble is with you lot is you're joke blind!

(Increasingly angry.)

Well here's something funny!

(He walks off to the side of the stage, finds a hammer and disappears behind the curtain. We hear banging and cursing. He emerges with a very mangled trumpet. Then tries to blow it.)

Sorry, it's a little flat.

*(**SPIKE** gets more and more manic.)*

I know you hate me! Well the feeling's mutual. Bloody Coventry! I hope you all get bombed again!

(He storms off stage. We may hear boos.)

SELLERS. *(To **SECOMBE**.)* I think he's depressed…

SECOMBE. **He's** depressed? I've got to go on next!

(We hear music strike up to cover the awkwardness. The spangly curtain rises…)

Scene Nine

(... To reveal the outside of **SPIKE**'s *dressing room door, number three. A star on the door and a handwritten sign saying 'Mr Milligan'.* **SELLERS** *and* **SECOMBE** *bang on the door.)*

SECOMBE. Open up Spike!

SELLERS. Come on Spike, it was just a bad audience, it happens. None of us got any laughs!

SECOMBE. Don't be a fool Spike, just open the door!

SELLERS. *(Adopting* **BLOODNOCK** *voice.)* Now listen to me Milligan, you're not to do anything silly. Do you hear me? Now that's an order!

(Back to normal voice.)

For God's sake Spike, just open the bloody door!

(No reply. They start to panic, and bash the door down with their shoulders. Finally the door gives way, to reveal **SPIKE** *standing on a chair with a noose round his neck, trying to hook it round an overhead pipe.)*

Good God!

SECOMBE. Don't do it Spike!

(Blue flashing lights. Ambulance siren.)

Scene Ten

(A hospital bed. **SPIKE** *is in it.* **JUNE** *arrives, clearly distraught.)*

SPIKE. It was a joke!

JUNE. Well it wasn't funny. Harry and Peter thought it was serious.

*(***SPIKE*** rummages by the bedside and shows* **JUNE** *a noose.)*

SPIKE. Look, it's a prop. The noose has a label – 'Only used once'.

JUNE. Hilarious!

SPIKE. You don't really think I'd kill myself for… Coventry?

JUNE. *(Humorlessly.)* Stop it Spike.

SPIKE. Come on love, I wasn't going to do it. Not that I'm scared of death… I just don't want to be there when it happens.

JUNE. For God's sake just stop!

SPIKE. I blame my mother – she was highly strung. She was hanging from the ceiling.

JUNE. STOP TRYING TO BE FUNNY! Everything isn't a joke! You've got to grow up and take your responsibilities seriously! You've got to think about someone apart from yourself. You've got a child. You can't **be** one!

*(***DOCTOR*** enters and gives* **SPIKE** *a sedative injection.)*

DOCTOR. This should help you calm down Mr Milligan.

SPIKE. Don't give it to me – give it to her! I'm perfectly calm.

DOCTOR. Go to sleep Spike. You'll wake up feeling much better.

> (**SPIKE** *closes his eyes, then wakes up with a start. We are still in a hospital but have gone back in time to the war.* **JUNE** *has gone. The* **DOCTOR** *now wears a military hat. We hear explosions off.*)

You've hurt your leg, Milligan, how are you feeling?

SPIKE. *(Stammering.)* I-I-I heard a b-b-big bang, then everything went b-b-bblack... now m-m-my head's just not right...

> (*Enter* **MAJOR JENKINS.**)

MAJOR JENKINS. Is he putting this on?

DOCTOR. I've listed him as suffering battle fatigue. He's a bit shaky and tearful now, but he will get better.

MAJOR JENKINS. I should bloody well hope so!

SPIKE. I-I-I j-j-just c-c-can't take it... the guns... the noise...

MAJOR JENKINS. We can't have you malingering. You've got to pull yourself together.

DOCTOR. I'm sure he will, given rest and...

MAJOR JENKINS. *(To* **DOCTOR.***)* Perhaps the sound of gunfire would improve his morale?

SPIKE. I-I-I c-can't stop crying. I don't know why.

MAJOR JENKINS. *(Loudly and slowly.)* Milligan – are you in a fit state to command men?

SPIKE. But, I ...

MAJOR JENKINS. Silence when you speak to an officer! Milligan, you were due a promotion, but under the circumstances, we're going to have to take away your stripe.

SPIKE. *(Incredulous.)* You're d-d-d-emoting me?

> *(Suddenly we are back in the present day. The* **DOCTOR** *disappears.* **SECOMBE** *and* **JUNE** *enter with flowers.* **SECOMBE** *has brought a radio.)*

SECOMBE. They're not demoting you, Spike... we're all just covering for you until you get better. Eric Sykes will finish off the scripts – you've done most of the work already – and we'll split all your voices up between us.

SPIKE. I bet you will!

JUNE. Everyone's being very kind, Spike.

SPIKE. What about the BBC?

SECOMBE. They want you to take as much time as you need to recover.

SPIKE. Of course. They are trying to get rid of me.

JUNE. You mustn't be paranoid.

SPIKE. Then tell them to stop trying to sack me!

SECOMBE. Nobody's trying to sack you. Look, Peter Eton's sent you a steam driven wireless! So you can hear exactly what's going on!

> *(***SECOMBE** *puts the radio by his bedside.)*

SPIKE. Who are they getting in as replacement?

SECOMBE. You're not being replaced, but they have to take measures to keep *(The show going.)* ...

SPIKE. Who is it?

SECOMBE. Just as a precaution – as a precaution, mind, we've got Dick Emery in.

SPIKE. Dick Emery? Are you serious?

SECOMBE. He can do all your voices... he's really very talented...

SPIKE. Will I still be paid? June's worried about how we're going to pay the bills.

JUNE. Of course I am. Someone has to be.

SECOMBE. Don't worry about that. I'll sort it out.

JUNE. Thank you Harry. That's incredibly generous.

SECOMBE. We've been through worse. Remember...

> (**SECOMBE** *starts singing* **["WHISTLE YOUR CARES AWAY"]**. *This time he is uninterrupted, so we get a real feel for how beautifully he can sing.*)

WHEN YOU'RE DROWNING IN THE WATER OF A SHARK INFESTED BAY
GIVE A LITTLE ...

> (**SECOMBE** *whistles.*)

... AND WHISTLE YOUR CARES AWAY.

> (**SECOMBE** *stops, uncertain as to whether he should continue. He carries on, singing more softly, and sincerely.*)

WHEN YOU'RE STANDING ON THE GALLOWS AT THE DREADED BREAK OF DAY
GIVE A LITTLE ...

> (**SPIKE** *whistles feebly.*)

... AND WHISTLE YOUR CARES AWAY

> (**SPIKE** *smiles wanly.*)

What's wrong with you? You're not trying to stop me singing!

SPIKE. I told you I was ill.

(**SECOMBE** *laughs and gets up to go.*)

SECOMBE. And if you are having trouble getting to sleep – the good news is *The Goons* is on later!

(**SECOMBE** *exits.*)

JUNE. *(To* **SPIKE.***)* I just want things to go back to normal. I just want you to be well again. No-one's forcing you to do anything. You can take your time...

SPIKE. I don't want anyone to think I'm shirking...

JUNE. Nobody thinks that... now get some rest.

(*She leaves.* **SPIKE** *turns on the radio. We see what he's listening to.*)

(*There is a knock on the door.* **SECOMBE** *answers as* **GENERAL SEAGOON***. We are suddenly in a Goon's sketch that* **SECOMBE** *and* **SELLERS** *are performing in front of* **SPIKE***, still confined to the bed, but without him.* **JANET** *in the background operates the spot effects.*)

GENERAL/SECOMBE. Come in, Major Bloodnok. Now, Bloodnok, you're a brave man.

BLOODNOK/SELLERS. Oh, yes, General Seagoon sir, I am. Why?

GENERAL/SECOMBE. Well, we want you to go on a very dangerous mission.

BLOODNOK/SELLERS. Dangerous?

(**JANET** *slams the door. She performs the sound of feet running off.*)

GENERAL/SECOMBE. *(Shouting off.)* You men over there! Try and catch him before he gets to the bus stop.

(We then hear the sound effect of feet running back. Door opens.)

BLOODNOK/SELLERS. Alright, General, I'm back.

GENERAL/SECOMBE. Why, Bloodnok, for a moment I thought you were turning coward!

BLOODNOK/SELLERS. For a moment I was. Once outside that door, though, I realised that I had to come back.

GENERAL/SECOMBE. Why?

BLOODNOK/SELLERS. I'd forgotten my hat. Goodbye.

*(We hear laughter and cheers from the **RADIO AUDIENCE**.)*

*(**SPIKE**, still in bed, doesn't know whether to laugh or cry.)*

SPIKE. *(Shouting at the radio.)* You dirty rotten swines! That should be me! How dare you do it so well!

*(**SPIKE** throws the radio to the ground. **PETER ETON** is the next visitor.)*

ETON. Don't worry about the show, we're surviving.

(He sees the smashed radio.)

Which is more than can be said for your radio...

SPIKE. It had a bit of a breakdown. I told it to pull itself together, but we're not on the same wavelength.

ETON. Are you all right Spike? You don't sound all right.

*(Pause as **SPIKE** considers this.)*

SPIKE. It's a terrifying feeling – knowing that you're tipping over the edge of sanity.

ETON. Perhaps we should revert to the original title – Crazy People.

SPIKE. I'm not acting crazy. I'm the genuine article.

ETON. The doctors tell me that the course of drugs and therapy are having a positive outcome.

SPIKE. You see? It's not just the Beeb. Even the loony bin wants to get rid of me!

ETON. Until they do, I've brought you something...

(He hands SPIKE a copy of Gargantua and Pantagruel, by Rabelais.)

Do you know *Gargantua*? By a french writer called Rabelais.

SPIKE. Rabelais?

ETON. He wrote fantasy, satire, grotesque bawdy jokes and songs. He's crude and scatalogical and very subversive – and inevitably incurred the wrath of the powers that be. Not surprisingly a lot of his books were banned by the Catholic Church... I thought it might appeal.

(SPIKE opens the book.)

SPIKE. Thank you Peter.

ETON. He was a great writer who thought the world was against him. He reminds me of someone. Can't think who.

SPIKE. The doctors don't allow flattery in here. We're meant to be coming to terms with reality.

ETON. The reality is I don't think the Goons can survive without you.

SPIKE. I don't know if that's true. But I do know that I can't survive without the Goons.

(The BBC EXECUTIVE calls from the other side of the stage.)

BBC EXECUTIVE. Peter... come and join me!

Scene Eleven

(BBC bar. **ETON** *joins* **BBC EXECUTIVE** *at the bar.)*

BBC EXECUTIVE. Did you catch the show?

ETON. Of course. I'm the producer.

BBC EXECUTIVE. No, no, *1984*. The Orwell Play. Your old drama department playing a bit of a blinder. Landmark broadcasting. A terrifying vision of the future. Big Brother, Room 101 and all that.

ETON. I sadly missed it. I hear it was very good.

BBC EXECUTIVE. More than very good, Peter. It's the programme the BBC was destined to make. It's what the BBC is for. What was it Lord Reith said was our mission? 'To Educate and Inform'.

ETON. You missed a bit off.

BBC EXECUTIVE. Did I?

ETON. 'To Educate, Inform and Entertain'.

BBC EXECUTIVE. Oh yes, that too. So all going well with the Goonies?

ETON. Yes. Everything's fine.

BBC EXECUTIVE. We've all heard about Milligan's unfortunate breakdown...

ETON. Due to Spike's... er... incapacity, we can't really confirm any kind of future schedule.

BBC EXECUTIVE. The thing is, Peter, not to put too fine a point on it... do you think he will **ever** be well enough to come back?

ETON. He's still in St. Lukes, but we just need to look after him for a while.

BBC EXECUTIVE. Yes, but we're not nursemaids, are we? And there have been a few demands that the programme be taken off the air. Rather a lot actually. Thirty, to be precise.

ETON. And I've defended it at every level...

BBC EXECUTIVE. Yes, all credit to you , but there does come a time when one has to recognise the reality of the situation.

> (**BBC EXECUTIVE** *moves closer for this conspiratorial tête-à-tête.*)

What I was thinking is that Sellers and Secombe are becoming big stars anyway and Milligan's chippy anti-BBC attitude hasn't made him any friends upstairs... so might now be the moment to pull the plug? Knock it on the head? Bring down the final curtain? You choose the metaphor... you're the creative bod... toodlepip.

> (**BBC EXECUTIVE** *leaves the bar.* **JANET** *appears with contracts for him to sign.*)

JANET. Cheer up, it may never happen.

ETON. I think it will. They want to kill off the Goons.

JANET. Surely they wouldn't do something as stupid as that?

ETON. How long have you been at the BBC?

Scene Twelve

> (**SPIKE** *is now sitting up in bed pleading with the* **DOCTOR** *who can barely look up from his paperwork. We are back in the war.*)

SPIKE. I want to go back. I want to rejoin the battery Sir.

DOCTOR/OFFICER. Don't be ridiculous. You burst into tears every time a door slams.

SPIKE. It's just the boredom. It's driving me... mad.

DOCTOR/OFFICER. That is rather why you're here with all the other PNs.

SPIKE. I'm not a psycho neurotic. I'm just a bit... loony.

> (**OFFICER** *laughs*)

I'm not a coward either. Let me go back. Give me another chance.

DOCTOR/OFFICER. You can't possibly fight but you can do your bit. I've heard you messing about on your trumpet and I gather you've a sense of humour. You're in no fit state for active service but you might just pass muster for light entertainment...

> (**SPIKE** *picks up his trumpet and with a burst of joy, plays a solo jazz piece which continues until a* **NURSE** *enters with his medication. We have moved from the War to the present day.*)

NURSE. (*Looking* **SPIKE** *in the eye closely.*) You're looking much better.

SPIKE. You're looking at the wrong end. My piles are killing me.

NURSE. You seem happier in yourself.

SPIKE. I am. Which is why I'm begging you, once again, please...

NURSE. No, Mr Milligan. It's for your own good.

SPIKE. All I want is... a pencil.

NURSE. We took away your pencils because we don't allow patients to have sharp objects.

SPIKE. It can be as blunt as you like! The trick cyclist says I'm getting better.

NURSE. He's not a trick cyclist, he's a psychiatrist.

SPIKE. Trust me...

NURSE. I really don't know about this...

(She holds a pencil, thinking.)

You won't do anything **silly** with it?

SPIKE. That's exactly what I'm going to do with it. I'm going to do something very silly indeed.

(He starts writing.)

(We hear the **[FLIGHT OF THE BUMBLEBEE]** *again, this time cranking up from slow to proper speed, before merging into* The Goon Show *theme.)*

Scene Thirteen

(The Goon Show theme continues. Three microphones on stands are picked out in spotlight. We are finally at a recording of the triumphant show in their greatest series.)

ANNOUNCER. This is the *Goon Show* on the BBC Home Service. Tonight we bring you a terrifying tale of the future. This is the story of the year Nineteen Eighty... Five! Big Brother is watching YOU!

(JANET at the spot effects desk bangs a large resounding gong. MILLIGAN, SELLERS and SECOMBE take their positions behind the microphones.)

MILLIGAN. The BBC would like to caution parents: this programme is unsuitable for the very young, the very old, the middle aged, those just going off, those on the turn, young dogs and Richard Dimbleby.

(JANET bangs the gong again.)

(We hear the sound effect of groaning, wailing and crying turning into screaming.)

SECOMBE/WINSTON. My name is eight-four-six Winston Seagoon. I am a worker in the great news collecting centre of the Big Brother Corporation, or as you knew it, the BBC. In every room is a TV screen that gives out a stream of orders.

SELLERS/BIG BROTHER. Attention people of England State. Thanks to the free market the price of tea has now gone down to eighty-five guineas a quarter. And here is good news for state housewives, the following goods are now in the shops: second-hand concrete parachutes; explodable woollen bloomers; men's self-igniting tail-less shirts.

MILLIGAN/ECCLES. Oh, it's good to be alive in 1985!

(We see **BBC EXECUTIVE** *and his wife* **MILDRED** *off stage listening to the wireless at home. He is smoking a pipe and she is knitting.)*

BBC EXECUTIVE. Oh for goodness sake! They are lampooning one of the BBC's finest productions.

MILDRED. Are you going to talk all the way through it dear? We might as well listen now it's on.

BBC EXECUTIVE. All I am saying is that they are comparing the BBC to some sort of dictatorship...

MILDRED. Shushh!

(We go back to the stage.)

SELLERS/BIG BROTHER. This is an announcement of special interest to Big Brother Corporation workers: The canteen is now open. Lunch is ready. Doctors are standing by.

(Back to the **BBC EXECUTIVE** *and* **MILDRED**. *She laughs.)*

MILDRED. That is quite amusing.

BBC EXECUTIVE. Shush – I am trying to listen.

(Back to the stage.)

SELLERS/BIG BROTHER. Worker Seagoon, did I hear you complaining about the BBC?

SECOMBE/WINSTON. Ohh no Big Brother *(Nervous titter.)*

SELLERS/BIG BROTHER. What is the finest TV Corporation in the world?

SECOMBE/WINSTON. *(Automatically.)* BBC TV.

SELLERS/BIG BROTHER. You are forgiven. As a penance you will put a copy of the *Radio Times* in your window.

(We hear sound effects sound of canteen hubbub, cups and saucers clinking.)

SECOMBE/WINSTON. As I sat at my table eating my boiled water I began to hate Big Brother Corporation.

SELLERS/POSH WOMAN. Winston darling, I have loved you from afar.

SECOMBE/WINSTON. My favourite distance. Who are you?

SELLERS/POSH WOMAN. I am six-one-two Miss Fnutt. I operate the Pornograph Machine in the Forbidden Records Department. And I love you!

SECOMBE/WINSTON. Now darling, where can we meet secretly?

SELLERS/POSH WOMAN. Somewhere where no one is listening.

SECOMBE/WINSTON. I know the very place. Home Service, eight thirty Tuesday night.

SELLERS/POSH WOMAN. You mean, the forbidden Goon Sector.

*(Back to **BBC EXECUTIVE** and **MILDRED** at side of the stage.)*

BBC EXECUTIVE. Oh really. Milligan won't let it go. Always complaining about the scheduling. Moan, moan, moan...

MILDRED. Oh do stop!

(Back to the stage.)

MILLIGAN/MORIARTY. Now then, Winston Seagoon, what do you know about television?

SECOMBE/WINSTON. I had three years at the BBC staff training college.

MILLIGAN/MORIARTY. What did you learn?

SECOMBE/WINSTON. Nothing.

MILLIGAN/MORIARTY. Good. We'll make you a director.

(Enter **SELLERS/BIG BROTHER**.)

SELLERS/BIG BROTHER. Eight-four-six Winston Seagoon. You are under arrest. You will be taken to room one-oh-one

SECOMBE/WINSTON. No! Not one-oh-one, not the listening room! Ahhh!!! Why are they strapping me in this box? Why these earphones?

SELLERS/BIG BROTHER. Begin the torture.

(We hear the theme tune to The Archers *which starts normally and gets faster and faster...*)

SECOMBE/WINSTON. No! No stop it! Stop it! Stop it! I can't stand it!

(Back to **BBC EXECUTIVE** and **MILDRED**.)

BBC EXECUTIVE. They have gone too far this time! Not the Archers! There must be some limits in a civilised society! And Mildred, will you stop laughing – it's not funny!

(**MILDRED** *ignores him.*)

MILDRED. It's nearly as silly as **you!**

(Back to the stage.)

BLUEBOTTLE. Enter top torturer Bluebottle, with junior cardboard cut out torture kit.

SECOMBE/WINSTON. (Appealing frantically.) No, Bluebottle, don't do it. Remember me? Your old pal Neddie Seagoon?

BLUEBOTTLE. ... You're the one who deads me every week, aren't you. Ehee hee hehe!! Thinks: I know the very thing for him. Prepares dirty big pile of dynamite for the dreaded deading of the traitor Seagoon.

> *(Back to* **BBC EXECUTIVE** *and* **MILDRED**.*)*

BBC EXECUTIVE. Oh no! He's not going to end the show with another explosion is he?

> *(We hear mighty explosion, falling rubble and metal.)*

MILDRED. Apparently so.

> *(On stage* **MILLIGAN** *registers his appreciation for the explosion to* **JANET**, *giving her a thumbs up. The action freezes as* **JANET** *takes centre stage.)*

JANET. That was a combination of an amplified version of Disc 19 Explosion – Ten Tons of Tri-Nitro Tolluine in a Welsh Quarry overlaid with Disc 23 – Demolition of a Large Industrial Tower, East Midlands, combined with a rather rare imported sound effects classic – Earthquake in Sumatra Richter scale seven. Afficionados will, of course, have detected amongst all of that structured soundscape a special recording of my own backfiring Morris Traveller.

> *(Beat.)*

I like to think that in the sound effects war one played a small part in Mr Milligan's victory.

> *(Beat.)*

Though you won't find me in the credits.

> *(Action resumes as* The Goons *theme tune comes up and we see the* **ANNOUNCER** *...)*

ANNOUNCER. That was *The Goon Show,* a recorded programme featuring Peter Sellers, Harry Secombe and Spike Milligan...

(**BBC EXECUTIVE** *turns radio off.*)

MILDRED. Well I thought the whole thing was...

BBC EXECUTIVE. A disgrace?

MILDRED. No. Very funny.

BBC EXECUTIVE. Really?

MILDRED. Particularly Peter Sellers. He's very dishy.

BBC EXECUTIVE. *(Annoyed.)* Not on radio he isn't! And anyway, it's Milligan who writes it all. He's the REAL talent, Mildred.

Scene Fourteen

(Radio Arts Studio. Two earnest men and an earnest woman discuss the show.)

CRITIC 1 (NOEL). It's three years since we last reviewed *The Goon Show* which in its last series seemed to reach new comedic heights. Roger, does it still tickle your funny bone?

CRITIC 2 (ROGER). Very much so. And Milligan's influence is extraordinary. He hasn't missed a show in seventy five episodes and his scripts manage to combine the satire of Aristophanes with the anarchy of the Marx brothers...

> (**CRITIC 1** *...while at the same time giving it a flavour of English music hall rewritten by Dean Swift...*)

CRITIC 3 (HERMIONE). ...with additional material by Kafka.

CRITIC 2. That's very good Hermione. I'm going to stick my neck out and say that their comedic oeuvre will be seen by history as very very significant indeed.

CRITIC 1. Although I personally don't think that this latest series is quite as good as the raw, unvarnished early work. To be frank, I liked it more when everyone else didn't.

CRITIC 2. Me too

CRITIC 3. Oh absolutely.

> (**CRITICS** *theme music plays which segues into party music.*)

Scene Fifteen

(BBC green room. It is the end-of-series party and the cast and guests are celebrating. We move around the party picking up different conversations.)

ETON. Congratulations Spike. That's the best series yet.

SPIKE. I expect you say that to all the series.

ETON. It's true. Seriously. Vintage Goons. Classics. Who would have thought it? You've now done more than a hundred and fifty shows…

SPIKE. I told you we should have called it the Go-on show. It goes on and on and on.

ETON. No-one's complaining Spike. You've got four and a half million listeners out there. You won!

SPIKE. In spite of the bloody BBC.

ETON. Because of the bloody BBC! They put us on, Spike. And they gave **you** something to fight.

SPIKE. They drive me mad.

ETON. You drive **them** mad. I'd say it was a partnership of equals. I take it back about you winning. It's a draw. The real winners are the listeners.

(The drink flows, brandy in abundance. A **FEMALE REPORTER** *is also at the party, with* **BBC EXECUTIVE.** *Music continues in the background.)*

FEMALE REPORTER. *(To* **BBC EXECUTIVE.***)* The BBC must be very proud of the Goons?

BBC EXECUTIVE. Oh yes. There's nothing the boys can't do. One-off Specials, novelty records… The Ying Tong Song, Walking Backwards To Christmas, Whistle Your Cares

Away… Yes, I have always been a great champion… spotted their potential right from the start…

FEMALE REPORTER. Really? And what about the treatment of the Royal Family?

BBC EXECUTIVE. We happen to know 'entre nous' that the Royal Family are actually huge Goon fans… The Duke of Edinburgh has invited the Goons to be his champions in the forthcoming Cambridge Tiddlywinks contest.

FEMALE REPORTER. What about the war? I know there were some complaints that they were being disrespectful?

BBC EXECUTIVE. The war? Not a problem, certainly not for ME. I particularly enjoyed their parody of the Bridge over the River Kwai – simply hilarious. *(Puts on bad Goonish voice.)* "We've got to blow up the bridge… we can't its got a puncture". You see, like a tyre…

> *(Away from the* **BBC EXECUTIVE**, **PETER ETON** *is now wearing a party hat, and is talking to* **SPIKE**.*)*

ETON. So is June coming?

SPIKE. No, it's mid-December.

ETON. You know what I mean.

> *(Pause as they both have a drink.)*

SPIKE. I think she's had enough of the Goons for a while. It isn't easy for her.

> *(***FEMALE JOURNALIST*** is still stuck with the* **BBC EXECUTIVE**.*)*

BBC EXECUTIVE. …oh no, we can take a joke against ourselves…the Goon parody of Orwell's 1984 with the BBC as the The Big Brother Corporation, was priceless!

(**SELLERS** *arrives.*)

SELLERS. *(To* **FEMALE REPORTER.***)* Is this man annoying you?

(**BBC EXECUTIVE** *laughs sycophantically.*)

I must save you at once!

FEMALE REPORTER. *(To* **BBC EXECUTIVE.***)* Sorry, I've got to be saved... excuse me!

(**SELLERS** *leads* **FEMALE REPORTER** *away, leaving* **EXECUTIVE** *on his own. He raises a glass to himself.*)

BBC EXECUTIVE. Well, here's to me!

(**SPIKE** *and* **SECOMBE** *have found a quiet corner amidst the debris of the spot effects table.*)

SECOMBE. Everyone seems very happy. Apart from you, obviously.

SPIKE. No, I'm **almost** happy.

SECOMBE. You should be. The scripts are the best you've ever written. Guaranteed roars of laughter, week after week. This is it, boyo.

SPIKE. Yes, I suppose it is.

(**SELLERS** *arrives with the* **FEMALE REPORTER.***)*

SELLERS. I found this delicious creature trapped by a marauding bore.

FEMALE REPORTER. Can I just get a few quotes from you all on the series?

SECOMBE. There's no way you'll get us to talk!

SPIKE. Unless you ask us some questions!

FEMALE REPORTER. You've been voted the funniest show on radio. You've had amazing reviews…

SELLERS. These questions are too tough… I can't take it any more…

FEMALE REPORTER. …no seriously… what does the success of the Goons mean to you?

SPIKE. Seriously… I think it might be my life's work.

> *(The others look at him, surprised at his sudden candour.)*

I'm just worried that my obituary will read: "he did the Goons and then he died".

FEMALE REPORTER. Would that be such a bad thing?

SPIKE. Ask me when I'm dead.

SELLERS. We can't let Spike have the last word – especially when he's being so… himself.

FEMALE REPORTER. OK, how do you hope people will remember the Goons?

SELLERS. Who?

SECOMBE. I hope they will remember it… as a time of hysteria and brandy, for soaring upward on the thermal currents of Spike Milligan's imagination, a time for wishing that every day of the week was a Sunday.

> *(Pause as they all take in this heartfelt tribute.* **SPIKE** *pats* **SECOMBE** *on the shoulder to say 'Thanks' in a reserved manner.)*

SPIKE. You grovelling little bastard!

Ends

(Chaotic music plays over curtain calls as **ANNOUNCER** *ends the show.)*

ANNOUNCER. That was 'Spike', a dramatic representation of the life and times of Terence Alan Milligan. And now it's time for the credits. The following have credited Spike Milligan and the Goons with being a major influence and inspiration:

Monty Python
Peter Cook
Dudley Moore
John Lennon
Private Eye
Dawn French
The Kumars
Robin Williams
The Muppets
David Bowie
Douglas Adams
The League of Gentlemen
Reeves and Mortimer
Stephen Fry
Eddie Izzard
King Charles... well, there's always one...
And many, many more...

(Music comes to an end.)

And this is me the announcer saying "This is me the Announcer".

Goodnight.

(Blackout.)

Ends

*(After the curtain call, **SECOMBE** begins to sing the Goons hit song* **[WHISTLE YOUR CARES AWAY]**. *The whole cast can join in, whistling and tooting.)*

SECOMBE.
>WHEN YOU'RE DROWNING IN THE WATER OF A SHARK INFESTED BAY
>GIVE A LITTLE ...
>
>>*(Sound effects: Whistle.)*
>
>... AND WHISTLE YOUR CARES AWAY

SELLERS.
>WHEN YOUR STANDING ON THE GALLOWS AT THE DREADED BREAK OF DAY
>GIVE A LITTLE ...
>
>>*(Sound effects: Whistle.)*
>
>... AND WHISTLE YOUR CARES AWAY

SPIKE/ECCLES.
>THE WORLD IS FULL OF WOE AND GRIEF, MISERY AND STRIFE
>BUT REMEMBER THIS REFRAIN AND IT IS SURE TO SAVE YOUR LIFE

SECOMBE SELLERS SPIKE.
>IF YOU'RE TIED UP TO THE RAILROAD AND THE TRAIN IS ON ITS WAY
>JUST GIVE A LITTLE ...
>
>>*(Sound effects: Trombone.)*
>
>... AND WHISTLE YOUR CARES AWAY!

Lightning Source UK Ltd.
Milton Keynes UK
UKHW021253280922
409584UK00015B/97